SUPER SERVICE

Also by Jeff Gee and Val Gee

The Customer Service Training Kit

SUPER SERVICE

Seven Keys to Delivering Great Customer Service
Even When You Don't Feel Like It
Even When They Don't Deserve It

Jeff Gee
Val Gee

McGraw-Hill

New York   San Francisco   Washington, D.C.   Auckland   Bogotá
Caracas   Lisbon   London   Madrid   Mexico City   Milan
Montreal   New Delhi   San Juan   Singapore
Sydney   Tokyo   Toronto

Library of Congress Cataloging-in-Publication Data applied for.

McGraw-Hill

*A Division of The **McGraw·Hill** Companies*

1 2 3 4 5 6 7 8 9 0 AGM/AGM 9 0 9 8 7 6 5 4 3 2 1 0 9

ISBN 0-07-024817-6

The sponsoring editor for this book was Richard Narramore, the editing supervisor was Fred Dahl, the editing liaison was Patricia V. Amoroso, and the production supervisor was Modestine Cameron. This book was set in Novarese by Inkwell Publishing Services.

Printed and bound by Quebecor Martinsburg.

Quantity Discounts Available

To order multiple copies of this book at a discount, please call the McGraw-Hill Special Sales Department at (800) 842-3075 or (212) 337-5043.

 This book is printed on recycled, acid-free paper containing a minimum of 50% recycled, de-inked fiber.

CONTENTS

INTRODUCTION

TOLL BOOTH

What are the benefits of delivering *Super Service* from a
customer service provider's point of view?

In the first draft of this book we included an amazing story. Marty, a tollbooth operator, takes *Super Service* to the next level by smiling and greeting every single driver who stops at his booth. We gave the story to a group of customer service providers who argued, "While we want to do a good job, we don't see any future in it, and we would never put our 'soul' into the job!" They joked that they didn't want to be an "eternally smiling tollbooth operator" and that people like Marty are extremely rare. This was great feedback, because it made us return to some basic questions:

1. From a customer service provider's point of view, what are the benefits of delivering *Super Service*?

2. How will it make the life of a service provider easier, more fun, more meaningful?

3. How will the book help providers who look at their jobs as *only jobs*, and who may be disillusioned, cynical, and tired of their work?

Not surprisingly, the answers to these questions are not based on the bottom line, productivity, or happy customers. They ultimately come from you, the customer service provider, because—wherever you go, whatever you do, however you feel—you cannot get away from yourself. This book is designed to help you find reserves of strength and joy in yourself that can help you enjoy giving super service to customers—even when you don't feel like it and even when they don't deserve it!

Think about it. It makes sense. Who gets to feel better after doing a good job? Who gets to experience fun when you make a customer laugh? Who gets to feel that work is more meaningful after helping a customer understand a system, learn something new, or grasp other things that your job consists of?

Your work as a service provider is critically important. A lot of research backs up this statement. That's why so many companies spend millions on marketing surveys that ask, "What do our customers want? How can we satisfy them?" The answers to these surveys are written up in customer service books directed toward marketing, sales, and management.

We, however, are more interested in how front-line customer service providers can deliver super service in a way that enriches their own lives, without feeling burned out at the end of the day. This book therefore defines the problems and answers that service providers—like you—come up against every day. We believe you can do a great job for yourself and your customers. *Super Service* is a positive philosophy on file.

If you don't believe it, read the story of Marty and ask yourself, "Does Marty feel good at the end of the day? Does it cost him anything? Does he make a difference in people's lives?" Here's Marty's story. See what you think!

Marty works on a very busy Illinois tollway and stands at the far left coin collection basket. His job is to watch cars go through, and that's what all the other operators do: just watch! Whatever the weather (and it gets below freezing in Chicago), Marty stands by the coin basket. Sometimes it's raining so hard he looks like a fisherman with all his wet gear on. What's different about Marty, though, is that thousands of drivers deliberately drive over 10 lanes of traffic just to go through his tollbooth.

Why? Well, if you keep your hand out after throwing in the coins, he gives you a high-five as you drive away. And if you whiz by without your hand out, he bends down, looks you in the eye, and calls out, "Hey, have a great day!" or "Make it a good one!"

We were so intrigued by him that one day we parked the car on the shoulder and walked over to him.

"Do you have a couple of minutes?"

"Well, I'm a bit busy," he said, nodding to the line of cars waiting to come through. (The barrier is left up in the mornings, so we weren't holding up traffic, but still …) "Sure!" he said.

We got right to the point: "How come you're always so cheerful in the mornings?"

"It's my job! *Have a good one!*" Marty called out, still attentive to his job.

"But all the other operators just stand there. They don't acknowledge a single driver unless there's a problem."

"It's their option in life, to do what they want to do. Mine is to be the best I can. I'm here to serve these people."

"Why?"

"I have to!" he said. Our blank faces told him we needed more information. "When I see all these drivers coming toward me looking so miserable and anxious, I feel it's my job to help them have a great day!"

"How long have you been doing this?" we asked, thinking Marty would say a year at most.

"Twenty years."

"And all that time you've been giving high-fives and saying, 'Have a great day!'?"

"Yep."

"Okay, trick question: Are you like this at home?"

"Yep."

Marty wasn't trained or asked to serve people; he just assumed the role—and thank goodness! If he weren't there, we'd really miss him.

Marty could have spent 20 years being miserable and thinking he didn't get paid to serve high-fives. His story is what *Super Service* is all about. It's more than putting yourself in the shoes of your customer. It's remembering that the customer is a human being, a person with a rent or mortgage to pay, kids to feed, a spouse, a mother, a father. A person with feelings just like you.

Marty could choose to think that his job is about working with a bunch of noisy, four-wheeled pollutants, that the line of cars coming toward him is just a never-ending machine. Instead he chooses to focus on the people within the cars; they are his customers. He recognizes their frustrations with the tollbooth: *They have to pay money to slow down!*

Marty has worked out that the best way to serve his customers is to make it worthwhile for them to slow down—even look forward to going through. His business proposition is that 40 cents is a small price to pay for the feel-good attitude he gives out. If you could talk with Marty, you would feel his self-worth. He's taken a job and upgraded it. He likes it and the customers like it. It's a win-win situation.

That's the story and, yes, being a tollbooth operator is not everyone's cup of tea. However, if you were a tollbooth operator, would you want to be the happy one? The one who made a difference? The one whom people remembered?

Marty represents what genuine service is all about: a person who cares about his job and believes his contribution can and will positively benefit others.

Perhaps your answer is still, "No! I wouldn't want to be happy in that job, because I might end up as a tollbooth operator for the rest of my life! I would rather be grumpy, miserable, and angry with the customers. Then my anger will force me to move on, or up, or somewhere else. Anywhere but here!"

The problem is that it doesn't usually work like that. Have you noticed that grumpy people stay grumpy even if they are in the best job in the world? So, if you are really unhappy in your job, do yourself and your company a favor: Change jobs.

But here's the kicker: Try delivering *Super Service in your current job* while you look for another one. Call it a practice session. If you can deliver great service when you really don't feel like it and they don't deserve it, your whole life will change. And that's really what *Super Service* is all about: serving yourself a great life.

So let's take a look at what *Super Service* can do for you:

How Super Service Works for Me

1. **I *experience being at my best*.** When I deliver *Super Service*, the person who receives the most service is me.

2. **I *am not at the mercy of my customers*.** It doesn't matter if my customers deserve *Super Service* or not; by choosing to give it to them anyway, I am in control of how I feel.

3. **My *life becomes easier, more fun, more meaningful*.** When I feed the positive energy within me, it grows in all other aspects of my life, and positive energy attracts positive energy! (The same is true with negative energy.)

4. **People *notice that I do a great job and I become an asset*.** When I am tired of my work or see my job as just a job, I really want to move on. The problem is that it's hard to move on when I feel stuck in mental fatigue. If I change my attitude, my whole world is filled with new opportunities.

Part I
THE BASICS

Chapter 1

THE HEART OF THE MATTER

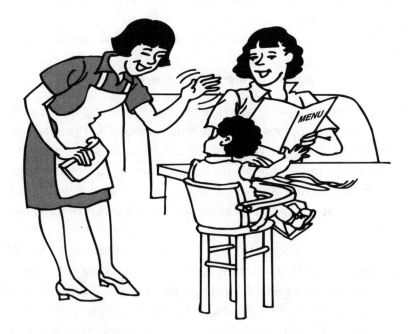

Connecting with a customer's heart and soul means experiencing
your customers as fully rounded human beings with all the joy,
family issues, money scares, and work problems that every one of
us experiences from time to time.

This book has everything you need to know about delivering great customer service.

One of the most important things you will learn is this: "My customer is anyone who isn't me." This lesson is so critical to you as a professional *Super Service* provider that it's worth repeating: **My customer is anyone who isn't me!** This definition of customers includes all the people inside and all the people outside your company: internal and external customers.

Too often, we think of customers as targets: people to be haggled with, sold to, or serviced like a washing machine. In reality, customers are people and people have relationships. How's this for a relationship builder?

Key Point
You may not always see your internal customers, but they are the people who benefit or suffer from the way you work.

Here's your drink, and I hope it chokes you!

This is a response from a fast food server who was fed up with a customer who dared to complain about the slow service. Did the server really hope the drink would choke the customer? Probably not; it was just a mindless thing to say. That's the problem with service: We get so bored that our mind goes off somewhere else, and when we do that, we stop being with the customer. Words tumble out of our mouths and, before we know it, we've created a situation.

If we served people the way we want to be served, we wouldn't have "situations." The problem is that most of us don't want to serve. "Serve" is a nasty word—something we did to make our way through high school or college. In the real world we think, *"It's not my job to serve people below me!"*

One of the many definitions of the word *serve*, however, is "to be of assistance, to help." Most of us want to help, but only if we are in the mood, if we like the person, or if we feel serving will advance our cause in some way. The secret weapon for fighting this attitude is to *wake up*.

You may say, "I am awake, so this doesn't apply to me!"

In the *Super Service* definition, "waking up" means being conscious of the fact that we are all in the *soup of life* together. It means opening our eyes wide in the morning and saying, "Yippee, I'm still on the planet!"

"Maybe certain people I hate most at work just reflect a negative behavior pattern that I hate in myself, and that's why I don't like being around them."

"Waking up" means asking yourself the question, "What if I change my attitude for a second and give that person a break?"

To give other people a break seems like a very hard thing to do; if we give them an inch, they might take a yard. Eventually that yard will turn into a mile and there'll be nothing left of me! Help! Where did I go?

Here's how waking up helps you: When you give someone a break, you are really giving yourself a break! Most of the time when we see a person we dislike, we think, "This person never smiles. He must dislike me a lot. I've seen him smile at other people." This thought gets louder over time. "*He never smiles at me. He must hate me, so I'm going to hate him back!*"

What happens then is really interesting. We become a mirror image of that person. We stop smiling at him, and we treat him as if he had the Ebola virus. In other words, we reflect his behavior back to him, and so the cycle continues.

Waking up means that we can break the cycle. We begin by noticing how we behave with other people. We notice that a person might just find it hard to smile, and we can decide to smile at the person anyway. If we don't get a response, it's okay because we want to be the kind of person who smiles.

What if *you* don't like to smile? Here's another example: "I hate that person because she always puts on a fake smile. She looks really dumb." When you see that person, you probably fake a smile back to her (and maybe even make an ugly face after she walks by). Again, it's a mirror image, and you end up with a fake smile plastered all over your face. So what do you do?

You could decide either to scowl at her or change the recipe: Speak to her. "Hey, I keep seeing you around and we've never met. I'd like to introduce myself." The moment you do this, you've woken up. You've broken the cycle of unfriendliness. It's a liberating feeling!

Domino's Pizza took the power of smiling to heart when they embarked on a new marketing campaign with a slogan, "A Million Smiles a Day." The campaign is grounded in simple, old-fashioned marketing fundamentals that say courtesy and friendliness go a long, long way. Domino's realized that their products, delivery, and services bring them face to face with many customers; so why not deliver a smile with every pizza!

Giver or Taker

Super Service professionals are great salespeople. They understand that to serve feels good and that it gets the job done. They have the attitude, "If I serve you, we both win."

You could say, "I don't get paid by commission. Why should I work harder and not get paid for it?" In a strict sense that response is true. You may not get more money today, but chances are that, when you change your pattern of behavior, everything will change, including your money. More importantly, you'll feel a whole lot better about yourself and your job.

Serving is about being a *giver* instead of a *taker*. If you think about it, we all serve other people. Even the most influential people in the world have to serve someone, even if it's a group of stockholders. Take a deep breath and hold it. Let the answer "pop" into your mind when you ask yourself this question: "Am I a giver or a taker?" Exhale. Whatever your answer, you get to choose how to react to this question. You can choose to think positive thoughts or negative thoughts. Here are some examples:

Positive Thoughts

I enjoy being a giver because I like to help people.

I enjoy being a taker because I like to receive.

Negative Thoughts

I hate being a giver because I don't get anything back.

I hate being a taker because people don't like me.

Sometimes, people take because they feel they have nothing to give. If your job is to answer customer complaints all day long, you need to give

> **Key Point**
> Don't think this book is about giving until you feel
> wiped out and have no strength left. We have to give
> to ourselves in order to give to others. It's a question of
> balance. *Take care of yourself, too!*

yourself breaks during the day. Revitalize your energy by taking a walk, reading a book, having a five-minute break to chat with a friend or colleague.

A client once asked us to support him by calling him an hour after lunch to remind him to take a break. But he never answered his phone, so we told his voice mail to take a break and hoped he listened to his messages before he went home!

We all need to take breaks. Here are 20 suggestions that will help you to revitalize your energy.

20 WAYS TO REVITALIZE YOUR ENERGY

1. Have a piece of fruit.
2. Drink a glass of water.
3. Stretch your neck very slowly, backwards, forwards, side to side.
4. Lift your legs and circle your feet clockwise and counterclockwise.
5. Write a letter to a friend.
6. Tidy your desk and/or drawers.
7. Empty your wastebasket and remove clutter from the floor.
8. View your space from a distance and make improvements.
9. Read a newspaper.
10. Read your company annual report.
11. Lift your shoulders to your ears, make them tense, then let go.
12. Take a short walk outside.
13. Take a bathroom break and walk a different route.
14. Hold your breath, then release all your tension.
15. Close your eyes and visualize your favorite spot to be.
16. Record an uplifting message on your voice mail.
17. Call your home phone and leave an uplifting message.
18. Start a journal and write a page a day.
19. Complete the sentence, "The insights I have about my life are … ."
20. Complete the sentence, "What I need to do to be happy is … ."

Everybody Serves Somebody

Question:	Who serves?
Answer:	Movie stars, *Super Service* providers, bankers, presidents, CEOs, kings; queens, generals, doctors, lawyers, etc., etc.
Question:	Do they feel their life is run by their customers?
Answer:	Probably at times, yes.
Question:	Do they ever get tired of their customers?
Answer:	Probably at times, yes.

We all serve and we all get tired of it. That's okay; it's *how* we serve most of the time that makes for a happy or an unhappy life. We might think, "I will serve this person, and sometimes another person, but I will never serve that person!" The problem with this kind of thinking is that we judge who gets served and who doesn't. What if we are wrong? On a purely material level, what if the person we would never serve becomes our boss? Do we leave the company?

Doesn't it make sense to be of service to whoever needs it at the time? (That isn't to say that we become the company server!)

The Cost of Losing a Customer

Did you know that 68% of customers are lost because an employee didn't handle their complaint well? The percentage is staggering but true! U.S. *News and World Report* found that:

- 1% of customers leave because someone in the company dies.
- 3% change location.
- 5% make other friendships.
- 9% go to competition.
- 14% are dissatisfied.
- 68% leave because of bad service!

It gets worse! Research shows that, out of 25 dissatisfied customers:

- One customer complains.
- Twenty-four are dissatisfied but don't complain.
- Six of the 24 noncomplainers have "serious" problems.
- The 24 noncomplainers tell between 10 and 20 other people about their bad experience.

From a pool of 25 customers, therefore, between 250 and 500 potential customers learn about the bad service.

These percentages work in exactly the same way on a personal level! If you are grumpy and unhelpful, most people will not confront you face to face. They'll simply tell other people about you, and pretty soon you're wondering why no one asks you out to lunch.

Here's an example of how easy it is to lose a customer. We have worked with Motorola for over 10 years; they are among our best customers. Some years ago, we got so much work from them that we became tired and irritable. We were scripting satellite broadcasts, writing training manuals, facilitating workshops, conducting pilot programs, producing videos, and doing much more.

To cover our growing workload, instead of hiring more staff (which is what Motorola assumed), we simply became overworked. We made mistakes, and that wasn't all. Because we had worked and partnered with Motorola for so long, we felt we had earned the right to complain. So we did!

One of the Motorola people with whom we were on friendly terms gave us fair warning. We were at lunch one day when the manager said, "I have to tell you that my people are looking at other vendors. They make their own decisions about who they work with and some companies cost less than you." Then the manager said bluntly, "If you don't change the way you do business, we may not be doing business with you anymore!"

Unbelievably, we still didn't listen. We felt so much a part of our customer that we considered ourselves bulletproof and, like lemmings, we jumped to our doom. Shortly after the warning, we handed a participant guide to one of their project managers. After finding some typos, the manager looked up and said, "So you haven't run it through spell check yet?" That was the day we lost our edge.

Finally, work from Motorola trickled to nothing and we got what we asked for—peace and quiet! We lost our best customer. Over the next year, our revenues dropped by 40%, and it almost cost us our business. It took another two years to find our competitive edge, bring Motorola back, and develop a bigger, more diverse customer base. It was an expensive lesson, but one we will never forget. Thank you, Motorola!

Maybe you're thinking that one lost customer won't have the same effect on you, because you don't have your own company. Wrong! Everything you do has a direct impact on your life.

Here's a positive story about a person who delivered Domino's Pizzas. The delivery person was in a hotel elevator delivering pizzas to the 15th floor, sharing the elevator with two other people. The three started talking and even got out at the same floor. A few minutes later, one of the people said, "How come you're delivering pizza? With your personality you should be a sales-person."

"This is my last week," said the delivery person. "I've just started working for a training company selling their programs."

"What kind of programs?"

"Selling skills, customer service, negotiating—they create a lot of different programs."

"We're looking for training in customer care right now," said the person. "I would be interested to hear more about your programs. Here's my card."

The delivery person is now one of our top salespeople, and we've been doing business with that client he met in the elevator for three years.

The point is that we never know who is a potential customer and how easy it is either to win or to lose a customer.

Take a look at Scandinavian Airline Systems (SAS). In 1981 SAS had done so poorly, it lost $8 million. Jan Carlzon, the president, researched the problem and found the lost revenues had nothing to do with airplanes, hangars, or standard operating procedures. Instead, he found that SAS was losing money because customers were unhappy!

Research showed that every time a customer comes into contact with an employee (baggage handling, flight reservations, etc.), the customer forms an opinion of the airline. Carlzon defined these experiences as "moments of truth." He calculated that every SAS customer has five "moments of truth" on each flight. Ten million customers represent 50 million opportunities to form a good or bad opinion of SAS! Carlzon decided that SAS needed to focus on customer care, and guess what? A little over one year later, the company turned an $8 million loss into a $71 million gross profit!

How did they do it?

- Managers served the front-line service providers so that they in turn could serve the passengers.
- Catering staff kept planes well stocked, so that flight attendants could assist passengers.
- Maintenance workers made it possible for flights to take off on time.

It seems almost too simple, doesn't it? Yet it's so obvious that major corporations often forget to do it. They don't focus on the customer's moments of truth. In fact, a friend of ours whose father was a maintenance worker for a large airline said they used to joke that "the gate should be renamed 'final assembly'!" Not the kind of comment that a customer would like to hear, is it?

How to Calculate Your Moments of Truth

This exercise will help you determine how many moments of truth you have with your customers each day.

MOMENTS OF TRUTH

- Take your mind back to yesterday at the very beginning of the morning.

- Make a checkmark in the space below for every time you communicated with a customer.

- Count up your checkmarks.

These are your moments of truth: opportunities to satisfy and retain existing customers, to interact with colleagues in a helpful manner, to build teams, and to manage people better.

Now recall the type of interactions you had. Close your eyes for a moment and remember your customers' faces, body language, and tone of voice. How did the interactions go?

SUPER SERVICE SELF-ASSESSMENT TOOL

Circle five words that most clearly show how you feel about your customers:

a. Interested	Empathetic	Informed
b. Problems	Issues	Jargon
c. Thanks	Clarity	Acknowledged
d. Ignored	Disinterested	Unclear
e. Green	Pleasant	Content
f. Disturbed	Red	Unpleasant

SUPER SERVICE SELF-ASSESSMENT RESULTS

1. Each row has a letter beside it.

2. Write down the letters that correspond to each of your circled words.

3. If three words or more appear on lines a, c, or e, *you enjoy interacting with your customers.*

4. If three words or more appear on lines b, d, or f, *you do not enjoy interacting with your customers.*

Don't worry about your scores too much at this point. You would not be reading *Super Service* if you didn't want to make some changes. The first step toward any kind of change is awareness. Congratulations! You have just made the first step.

Connecting Heart and Soul

Connecting with a customer's heart and soul means experiencing your customers as fully rounded human beings with all the joy, family issues, money scares, and work problems that every one of us experiences from time to time.

To connect with a customer "heart and soul" takes no more than standing in front of a mirror and looking at yourself. Do it! Go to a mirror, and you will see before you a customer! How does it feel? How do you act as a customer? If you have an argument with your beloved, do you allow it to ring in your ears all day? Or do you still manage to behave as a great customer?

Chances are that, if you aren't a great customer, it will be a push for you to give *Super Service*. Try the following exercise:

- Take a moment to sit quietly and relax.
- Inhale one deep breath.
- Hold it.
- Ask yourself, "Do I treat my customers as I like to be treated?"
- Exhale.

Every person is a customer at some time or another. Put yourself into your customer's frame of mind. How do you as a customer like to be treated? To help you gauge your attitude, complete the special checklist on the next page.

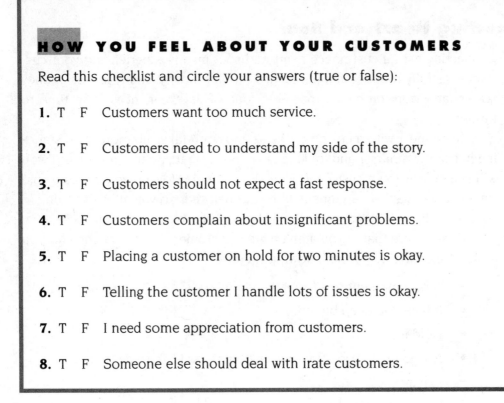

HOW YOU FEEL ABOUT YOUR CUSTOMERS

Read this checklist and circle your answers (true or false):

1. T   F   Customers want too much service.

2. T   F   Customers need to understand my side of the story.

3. T   F   Customers should not expect a fast response.

4. T   F   Customers complain about insignificant problems.

5. T   F   Placing a customer on hold for two minutes is okay.

6. T   F   Telling the customer I handle lots of issues is okay.

7. T   F   I need some appreciation from customers.

8. T   F   Someone else should deal with irate customers.

ANSWERS

The answers are written as if you are the customer. This way you will understand the point of view from a customer perspective.

1. FALSE   Customers want too much service.

As a customer yourself, you want and expect good service; there's no such thing as too much.

2. FALSE   Customers need to understand my side of the story.

You are concerned with your own problems, especially if the service provider is responsible for them. You are not interested in their side of the story.

3. FALSE   Customers shouldn't expect a fast response.

As a customer, you may have tried to solve the problem yourself. By the time you've called the service provider, you've already spent too much time on it and you expect a fast response.

4. FALSE   Customers complain about insignificant problems.

*No problem is too small to a customer. If you have a problem and the service provider tells you it's insignificant, how does it make **you** feel? Very frustrated!*

5. FALSE   Placing a customer on hold for two minutes is okay.

Close your eyes and get someone to tell you when a minute is up! What were you thinking and feeling as the time went on? Putting anyone on hold for longer than 30 seconds may lead to damaging thoughts.

6. FALSE   Telling the customer I handle lots of issues is okay.

As a customer I interpret this to mean that the product or service is prone to lots of problems. Not good for long-term business!

ANSWERS (cont.)

7. FALSE   I need some appreciation from customers.

What goes around comes around, and we all like appreciation. Often that appreciation comes from a different source. Customers are not always appreciative, even of good service; they expect it!

8. FALSE   Someone else should deal with irate customers.

Have you ever been an irate customer? If so, you probably know that you are usually annoyed at the product or the company, not the person serving you. But if that person starts to take it personally, you feel the tension build. So, from either point of view, don't take things personally.

Positive Energy

Julia works for a large store and is one of their top salespeople. Why? Julia loves people. Walk into the place and she smiles just because you've walked in. It's not a "fake" smile, either—she is a "Marty high-five" kind of person. People want her to serve them. She raises the pleasure level of buying just by showing the delight that you've walked into the store. Whether you are a new customer or a regular, Julia has the same high level of energy.

Also, Julia knows the product. She makes practical suggestions. Of course, we buy more than we went in for, but it's so much fun, it's okay! We don't even get the usual buyer's remorse.

Julia connects heart and soul with her customers. She has the desire to serve: "Oh I'm so glad you came in. I've missed you! It's so good to see you!" Okay, on the printed page the reaction may sound like too much, but with the brightness and the smile it's a winner.

And who benefits? Everyone! The store, the customer, and, of course, Julia. She enjoys her job, and she does it well. She's acknowledged by her colleagues, she's on first-name terms with top management, and she's rewarded monetarily: Julia has been promoted and given a raise!

Can everyone do it the way she does? No. We may not have her particular brand of charisma! What will work just as well is a willingness to serve and be served. Ever been in your local food store and stood at the checkout? Are you a great customer? Do you ask the clerk if he or she is having a good day? Does the clerk need a smile? Just like Marty at his job, the clerk can stand there or just *stand there*!

Consider Jim. Before he understood the what-goes-around-comes-around principle, he was a rotten customer and a rotten server. He demanded things as a customer, and gave little as a server. So what did he get in return? Demands and little else! He was treated with horror and fear. Did he get what he wanted? Usually not. When he did, it never felt right. Jim lived in a war zone. Then he went to a training workshop and had a breakthrough! To be great at *Super Service, even when he didn't feel like it, even when customers didn't deserve it*, he had to be a great customer himself.

Jim learned that we all serve and are served every day of our lives, that our attitude is the important part. Much of our lives is determined by the tone of the script we write for ourselves: We can choose comedy, drama, tragedy, or romance. It's our choice!

Super Service Workouts

On the next page are some *Super Service* affirmations. Pick one to use each day.

SUPER SERVICE AFFIRMATIONS

1. My *customer is anyone who isn't me.*

2. My customers are people first.

3. I am a great customer.

4. I take full responsibility for solving customer problems.

5. I keep all the promises I make to my customers.

6. I establish and maintain good rapport with customers.

7. I respect my customer's point of view.

8. I listen to understand how my customers feel.

9. I look beyond their words to understand their feelings.

10. I always acknowledge what my customers are feeling.

11. I show a desire to serve.

12. I smile and maintain eye contact.

13. I sit straight and I stand straight.

14. I will not "give away the shop" to bribe customers.

15. Every interaction is a positive attitude opportunity.

16. I control my biases and my judgments.

17. I show my customers that I care and am on their side.

18. I acknowledge my customers' priorities.

19. I take responsibility and use "I" instead of "we."

20. I connect with my customers "heart and soul."

CHECK-IN

You know who your external customers are, but do you know your internal customers and how your job affects theirs? Make a list of the internal customers that your job most affects: include the boss, colleagues, peers, assistants, different departments or locations. Use the example as a guideline:

Internal Customers

Michelle Somers

How My Job Affects Theirs

Updating address and phone info

ACTION: HOW AM I DOING?

Read the following statements and circle "yes" or "no."

Yes   No   I show a desire to serve.

Yes   No   I am a problem solver.

Yes   No   I recently helped solve a difficult problem.

Yes   No   I gather information well.

Yes   No   People understand the information I give.

Yes   No   I check for understanding.

Yes   No   People feel comfortable asking me for help.

Yes   No   I am a considerate customer.

Yes   No   I give more than I take.

Yes   No   I would enjoy being served by someone like me.

ACTION: HOW AM I DOING? RESPONSE

- Go back a page to the exercise and count up the number of "yes" responses and the number of "no" responses.

- If you had six or more "yes" responses, you are already understanding what *Super Service* is all about.

- Six or more "no" responses indicate some areas that you could improve on. Use the space below to write one main area for improvement:

- My main area for improvement is _____

- I will improve this today by _____

Chapter 2

SERVING UP YOUR BEST (EVEN WHEN FEELING YOUR WORST)

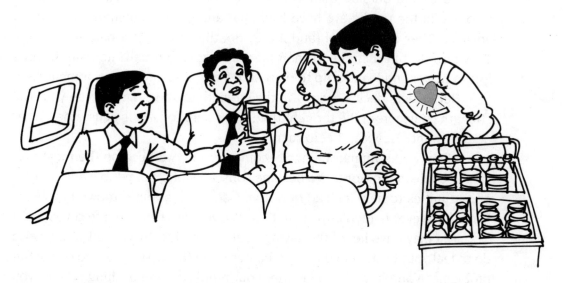

To serve others is to ultimately serve ourselves because,
when we open our hearts, our spirit grows and becomes stronger.

When you feel great, serving is fairly easy, but it's very difficult when you feel depressed or have major problems in your life. Fortunately, showing a desire to serve is a skill that can be learned, no matter how bad you are feeling.

What if you believe that showing the desire to serve means becoming a doormat? All others want to wipe their feet on you: Get me that! Bring me this! Do it now!

In truth, the opposite happens. Serving takes great courage, power, leadership, and a strong spirit. To serve others is ultimately to serve ourselves because, when we open our hearts, our spirit grows and becomes stronger. Here's how you do it:

1. Put your own feelings backstage for a short while.

2. Focus on the customer.

3. Bring them to frontstage in your mind.

4. Take care of their needs.

Think of the great courage it takes to serve. Think of anyone in the public eye: presidents, first ladies, kings, queens, supermodels, Grammy award winners, and so on. Public figures, as humans, experience illness, family crisis, and events outside their control. Yet, unlike us lesser-knowns, people who live in the public eye have lives that are arranged sometimes years in advance. They can't cancel (and if they do, they soon get a bad reputation). They have to put a smile on their face and move through the pain. It takes lots of power and leadership to do that. It's much easier to stay home in bed.

But leaders decide they have the strength to serve, and so can you. The strength comes from the thought that, "I am here to help my customer. What do they want? How can I help them?"

When we as human beings become servers, we become the most precious people in the world. We become conscious of other people and look for opportunities to help instead of worrying so much about our own problems. If you have ever helped anyone in this way, you know how uplifted you feel.

You may have heard the saying, "Let go, let flow." That's all you have to do to feel your best. Let your mind be free of all the chatter. Let go of all your problems, worries, and ego, and let your mind become nothing so that you can be everything for your customer.

When you are being your best, you feel in alignment with all that is good about life. You are in touch with an inner strength that enables you to turn off the little voice in your head that says you aren't good enough, or thin enough, or fit enough, or good-looking enough, or smart enough, or wealthy enough, or "enough" of anything!

Being your best means accepting yourself as you are right now! It means that you wouldn't change a thing. Sometimes, when we look back at our lives, we remember things we have done or not done, things that, with our current wisdom, we think we could have done better. Because we are older and wiser, we think, "What a mess I made of my life!" If only I had studied more, had different friends, had a better family, etc.

We can change this way of thinking by repeating the following phrase: "I am the best, and I'm getting better and better every day!" It almost sounds too simple, but sometimes the simplest things are the most effective.

You may be thinking, "I have a life, I don't want to bring my customer to frontstage and put myself backstage!" Yes, it's true, you do have a life. If part of your life includes working with customers, why not accept it? When you do, magical things happen and your own life becomes much easier.

It's like this: Water is wet, rocks are hard, and customers want to be served. Depending on our job, we call customers by different names: fans, constituents, loyal subjects, clients, patients, etc. They all expect service, so why not serve them? Make it easy for yourself to help them; get into the flow of delivering *Super Service* and discover how fresh it feels to do a great job! All we suggest is this: If your job is to serve customers, maybe you can empty your mind of some of your own things and leave a little space for them.

HOW TO SHOW A DESIRE TO SERVE

1. **Be in control of your attitude.** If you wake up with a bad attitude or something triggers it during the day, become an actor for a while. Think of a person who has a positive attitude. See him or her in your mind. Imagine how the person sits, stands, walks, and talks. Feel yourself become like that person.

2. **Let your anger go.** Anger is poisonous and feeds on itself. If anger comes up, simply take a deep breath, hold it for a count of three, then let it go. Feel the anger release with the breath. We breathe not just to bring in oxygen, but to release carbon dioxide. Let your anger go with your exhale.

3. **Maintain a positive attitude.** If you want to feel satisfied in your job and experience energy and fulfillment at the end of your day, have a positive attitude. Think good thoughts. Do the right thing. Make the best choices.

4. **Affirm your day.** When you wake up in the morning, brush your teeth, look at yourself in the mirror, say out loud, "Today is going to be a great day. No matter what I am doing, I am going to do it with the desire to serve. I will be positive, upbeat, and ready to be the best for my customer!"

Step Outside Yourself

By serving only the "worthy" customers, you shut out the majority of people. Let's face it: Most people are not like us. They don't look like us or act like us. If we were all the same, there wouldn't be newspapers, or books, or articles, or TV programs, or movies.

In Victorian times, we used to have the "deserving" poor. These were the people who had no money, but still swept their mud floor and kept themselves as clean as possible. The "deserving" poor got help from charities. The "undeserving" poor were the dirty, unkempt people who didn't look as though they deserved help. Every time we treat customers in a lessened way, because we feel they are "undeserving," we step backward. We need to step forward. Being at your best means celebrating the differences, enjoying the interesting and different styles of people. Show a desire to serve everyone with equal skill and wisdom.

Most of the time, we are too busy in our own little world to really see the people around us. We meet people for the first time, and after a couple of seconds we have categorized, labeled, and placed them in a box. Some people get put in boxes never to be seen again, and these people could be your best allies in the customer care cycle.

We might prefer to rub elbows with people who look smart and wear the right clothes, but they may also be too busy to help you in a crisis with a customer. If we can just stop our judgments about people—let them be our teachers, accept them for the wonderful people they are, with all their quirks and strange little habits (because, of course, we don't have any)—we would be more than halfway to providing *Super Service*.

On the coming pages are affirmations and exercises that may help you to step outside yourself and find a role model, a teacher, or a mentor.

AFFIRMATION LIST

Everyone is my teacher.

I am in touch with my feelings and can relate them to others.

I learn from everyone around me.

I am awake and help others to awaken.

I am objective about people.

I am open to every different kind of person.

I see the potential in everyone.

I let go of my fear about people and accept them all as they are.

I look to a mentor as a wise and trusted counselor.

I value serving others.

Take Responsibility for Your Mistakes

We were having a plumber do some work. He was supposed to have the job finished by the time we came back from a short business trip. We explained that we would be returning with a visitor, so the bathroom had to be finished.

Of course, it wasn't done. The bathroom was all ripped apart. The tiling was uneven and a single pipe was sticking out of the wall. Plaster lay in the bath and on the floor. It was a mess!

The plumber gave us a long story about a bad tooth with a complicated sinus infection that led him to the hospital. His head was hung, and his eyes flitted right and left like a pendulum. He didn't sound as though he was telling the truth.

"How was your trip?" he asked in an attempt to divert the attention from him. Needless to say, it did not work.

"When can you finish it?" we asked.

"Probably Thursday."

"Thursday! Definitely?"

"Yes!" he said.

He finished the main part of the job on the Friday, and finished off other things over the next few weeks.

Will we ever use him again? No! Does it matter to him? Yes! He certainly won't get a good reference from us, and we will call the company that referred him and tell them what happened. More importantly, he did not feel good about himself.

If we cannot look our fellow human beings in the eye and maintain a clear and steady gaze, there is something wrong! If we do not feel that we did a good job, then we need to accept responsibility for that. Here are a few simple things that help you take responsibility:

HOW TO TAKE RESPONSIBILITY

1. **Make "I" statements.**

   "I will call the service department."

   "I will look into that and get back to you by next Monday."

2. **Complete things.**

   Make a list of things you need to complete. It could be as simple as writing to a friend or a parent. Then get those things done!

3. **Take notes.**

   If you don't write down what you said you will do, it may never happen.

4. **Keep your word.**

   If you have ever been stood up or had someone change plans on you at the last minute, you know how bad it feels. Keep your word, and people will keep their word with you.

Super Service is about you. How you treat people is how others will treat you. If you take time and care with people, they will take time and care with you. Super Service doesn't mean that you are doing everything with an ulterior motive, that if you do something for someone, you expect it back threefold. It may never come from the person you expect it to come from, but it will come.

ACTION

Next time you are with a customer (either internal or external), evaluate yourself on how you are doing. Here's a very short list of questions to answer:

1. Was I honest?

2. Did I complete the task?

3. Did I help the situation?

4. Did I show a desire to serve?

Super Service is about you caring about you. It's about feeling good at the end of the day. You can start right now, today. Keep an eye on yourself by asking, "Am I conscious of what I am saying, what I am doing, and how I am doing it?"

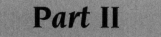

Part II

SEVEN KEYS TO DELIVERING SUPER SERVICE

Chapter 3

CUSTOMER SERVICE KEY 1
THE RIGHT ATTITUDE

Seeing the good in yourself and your circumstances is an important step in having a positive attitude.

There are seven basic keys to delivering great customer service. Together, these keys form a flow of communication between you and your customer. Keeping this flow smooth will help you and your customer by lessening the conflicts and anxiety caused by miscommunication. When you are "in the flow," your job will run more smoothly and you will find it more enjoyable.

Getting into the flow always begins with Customer Service Key 1: having the right attitude. Whether you are reaching agreement, checking understanding, or taking action, having the right attitude is always the first and most important key to *Super Service*.

The easiest way to show the importance of this first key is to give you an example of someone who did *not* have it:

Each of us has held a life insurance policy for over 10 years with one insurance agent. We never hear from him unless the rates change. Recently, he sent literature that caused us to look at buying a 20-year fixed-rate policy from him. Over the course of a week, our agent spoke to each of us at separate times, so we both received slightly different information.

When we had time to sit down and look at the two policies, we saw that we'd be paying an extra $500 for the first year. When we called to ask him about it, he didn't want to listen. This is how it went:

"John, we noticed that we will be paying $500 more for the first year."

"Have you done your blood test to qualify you for the new policy yet?" he replied, ignoring the question.

"Not yet. What about the premium?"

"The blood test has to be done by next week," he continued, still ignoring the question.

"What about the premium?"

"We already discussed it."

"Not with me!"

"I discussed it with your partner," he replied gruffly. "If you don't get your blood work done soon, you will miss the window of opportunity!"

John failed to keep our trust by not having the right attitude. He didn't answer our questions and he used manipulative tactics to get us to buy a different policy. Well, guess what? We ended up wanting to miss the window and, to cut a long story short, we no longer felt loyalty to this agent. We looked for another policy with a different agent and will definitely not recommend him to anyone else.

You might think you have to do lots of things to get the right attitude. But the strange thing about having and maintaining the right attitude is that it starts with *taking away*, not *adding to*.

Next time you are with a customer (either internal or external), empty your mind of everything except that person. Stop your thoughts and allow yourself to be in the same space with them. Stop thinking about your next task or your project deadline. Allow yourself to become still, just for a moment or two, and let the frenzy of your world continue without you. This is the "taking away" process; you "take away" all distractions.

When we listen to our internal dialogue instead of to the person who is talking, we might as well be at home sleeping, because we are certainly not there for them. We want them to talk faster, so that we can get on with the important stuff—which usually translates to *our* stuff. We hate the joke or the story that we heard last week or even the week before. We don't have time to listen about their children, spouse, finances, or health problems. "We have real work to do, for goodness sake!"

If we're in the business of customers, if we work with people, if people are in our life, we need to take time to listen—with a positive attitude. We need to empty ourselves of our own immediate concerns and focus our complete attention on serving the customer.

Maintain a Positive Frame of Mind

We were sitting at a sidewalk cafe when an elderly man nodded toward our table and asked, "Are we all happy?"

"Yes," we chorused. He smiled and walked on. We recognized him as W. Clement Stone, one of the founders of Positive Mental Attitude. He is probably a millionaire many times over, yet this elderly man still takes the time to ask a bunch of strangers if we are all happy!

There was no reason for him to bother about us. We weren't customers, friends, or even neighbors. There was nothing visible in it for him except that he is obviously bright and alert to everything going on around him. He makes the choice to be happy, and it touches everyone around him.

Most of us tend to think happiness is elusive—something we've left behind or something we are working toward. But happiness is *right now*. It's waking up to a dark cloud-filled sky and going on the picnic anyway.

Let's say you have a lousy job. You're underpaid. Your colleagues are different or even seem strange to you. You have to work an 11-hour day. The person at the next workstation is a grouch. Your boss hates you. No one asks you to lunch. The customers are all demanding. The product is terrible. You don't have a corner office. You do have a corner office and you feel left out. The elevator takes hours, and on and on.

You may think, how can I possibly be happy? If I look at my life realistically, I will probably shoot myself in the foot just to get sick leave! There is no way I can have a positive frame of mind. I would be mad to enjoy this situation.

The reality, however, is very different. You have a job! Hallelujah! In a world where poverty and famine are a constant, having a job is a real bonus. You still hate it? Then work like crazy to get another one. Still do your work, be the best you can be, and look for another job. Get a great resume together. Hunt the newspapers. Ask friends. Get a head-hunter. Go to a career counselor. Make your focus a new job.

Then understand one thing: You will have equally annoying people and situations in your new job. Why? Because until we see how good we are, we will not recognize the hidden good in other people. Seeing the good in yourself is an important step toward having a positive attitude.

Once, during a sermon about happiness, the speaker had some great tips and introduced them all with such phrases as, "This may sound dumb but ..." or "I know this seems crazy ... ."

Why? Why do we think it's crazy to smile even though we feel like crying? Or to read an uplifting book, or listen to wonderful music, or do any of the things we can do to uplift our spirit?

Having a positive frame of mind is hard only if we want it to be hard. If having a hard life is easier to us, then we will interpret having a positive frame of mind as being hard, because that's the way we want it to be!

"But I'm not a happy and outgoing person," you say? Not so. We all have the potential to be whoever we want to be. All it takes is a little positive energy. Instead of being a drain, decide to be a filler-up. Tell yourself, "I will fill my life with joy. I will give. I will serve. I will do whatever is necessary to get the job done."

Our training and consulting business demands a lot of airline travel. The best airline we have ever used is Singapore Airlines because the employees go beyond their duty. They actively look for problems and often see them before they even arise: parents with children needing extra hands, frail people with heavy luggage, nervous first-timers who don't see their seat numbers. It's wonderful to experience people who have this desire to serve.

If we didn't have so many frequent flyer miles racked up with the airline we usually fly with, we wouldn't use them because we are treated like cattle. Once two parents were boarding the flight with their three young children, two strollers, and one set of luggage wheels. The mom went first with a child and a stroller. The dad struggled with the rest. The flight attendant simply stood there and told him where he *could not* put his stroller or luggage wheels. The flight attendant was obviously very angry at the passenger for being a parent and having baby gear to be stowed away. This irritated the father, set the children off, and got all the surrounding passengers in a tizzy, as some sided with him and others with the flight attendant. As the flight was being attended to in the cockpit, there was chaos back in the "people pit."

We wondered how Singapore Airlines flight attendants would prepare for their day. Maybe something like this:

1. **Prepare yourself.** Before the passengers come on board, prepare yourself for every event.

2. **Think about why you are here.** Look for opportunities to help.

3. **Pay attention.** Look for people in need: elderly, parents with young children, people with physical disabilities, and nervous first-timers.

4. **Maintain a positive frame of mind.** Look for ways to make a positive difference.

This is about you. How you feel at the end of the day is determined by keeping a positive attitude through the rough times. The only way you can do that is to be the best you can be, not to take things personally, and keep smiling.

Even if you start the day with a positive frame of mind, your feeling of well-being can slip away as the day wears on. This is when many people allow their positive attitudes to slip away also; however, this is exactly the right time to think differently. You are responsible for being in control of the way you act and live your life.

If you feel depression or anger coming on because of how a project has gone or because of something someone said, don't do what you normally do (like take your frustrations out on a sympathetic person, spouse, or coworker). Instead, take a few moments to breathe. Take a walk outside or to another part of the building. Sip a glass of water to cool down (not coffee, you don't need to feel more jittery!). Have some uplifting words handy to read. In other words, physically take action to lift your mood.

When you are feeling down, that's *exactly the time you can make a difference*! You are responsible for you. Nobody else can do it for you. You deserve to be happy. You deserve to have a positive frame of mind. You deserve to be the best that you can be! Here are some exercises to help you maintain the right attitude.

AFFIRMATIONS FOR MAINTAINING THE RIGHT ATTITUDE

1. I want to help.

2. I'm happy to make a difference.

3. I maintain a good, positive frame of mind.

4. I am always prepared.

5. I am sincere.

6. My energy is uplifting.

7. I take time to breathe and control my response.

Thoughts to Avoid

You know them already—so we won't even highlight them!

CHECK-IN

We learn by example. Make a list of people who manage to keep a positive attitude, even when they're tired. Ask yourself these questions:

1. What is it about them that makes them seem so positive?

2. Are they more outgoing?

3. Do they smile more?

4. Are they giving?

5. Do they go with the flow?

6. Do they make an effort to go forward with a better attitude?

7. When they are angry, do they get rid of it quickly?

8. If someone insults them, do they take it personally or shrug it off?

ACTION

Which skills do *you* need? How can you learn these skills? If you need to smile more, do it. If you need to take things less personally, do it. Walk past a group of people and say, "Are we all happy?" But here's the test: You have to say it with sincerity, as if you really want them to be, as if you are sharing your happiness with them.

Chapter 4

CUSTOMER SERVICE KEY 2
UNDERSTAND THE CUSTOMER'S NEEDS

Imagining what it is like to be your customer is a powerful customer service technique.

Other people's shoes rarely fit. If we want to understand people better, we have to make allowances. Have you ever been told to "put yourself in their position" or "stand in their shoes"? What does it really mean?

Understanding someone else's experience is impossible unless it has happened to us, and even then the experience will be different. What we can do, though, is imagine. Imagining what it is like to be your customer is a powerful customer service technnique. It's a first step toward understanding the customer's needs.

Prepare for a Customer Interaction

Another more concrete trick for understanding customer needs is to keep a file for each of your external customers. Use the files (or your company's existing files for customers) to hold information that will help you remember them and understand their past problems and concerns. This will help you understand their needs better during your next conversation. Before a meeting, review the file and get to know the customer's product or service history. Understand past problems, recommendations, and solutions.

In our experience, there's nothing worse than service providers who have not done their homework before talking to a customer. A woman friend told us about a recent experience when her doctor asked, "Everything okay with your period?" "I had a hysterectomy two years ago!" she replied. This does not make for a good doctor–patient relationship. We can be effective only when we have done our customer homework. In the example of the doctor and patient, the information must have been in the patient file. Why didn't the doctor take time to read it? Being "too busy" is not a good answer. How can service providers ask the right questions when they have the wrong (or no) information?

Is it different for people who deal with a large number of unknown customers each day and who do not form long-term personal relationships? Yes and no. Obviously, we cannot know personal details of customers we may speak to only once every two months. What we should know, however, is:

1. Typical problems and how to resolve them.

2. The options available to our customers.

3. Past case histories.

Preparation means knowing in advance what might come up. It doesn't take long to do, but in terms of *Super Service* it is time very well spent.

How to Listen with an Open Mind

An open mind is one that is open to new experiences and new ideas, like an empty vessel ready to be filled. (Remember that, by being "no thing," you can be "every thing" for your customer.) Listen to your customer's problem with an open mind, and, as you listen, fill your mind with the problem. Only when you have the complete problem should you begin to think of a solution.

Unfortunately, the mind is so resistant to remaining empty and being filled with another person's problem that it fills itself up with solutions. Then, desperately wanting to pour itself out, the mind overwhelms listeners with a "flash flood" of solutions.

So how do we retain an open mind? How do we remain open to listening to our customers, to really hear what they are saying before we interrupt and drown them out? Here is a visualization technique to follow when talking with a customer.

When you are steering the boat, you have the power to take it wherever you want to go. The customers can row and row and use up as much energy as they want, but they cannot get to their destination without you steering there. But the object of steering is to land safely—by solving the customer's problem. It is a huge responsibility and you need to have some skills—in your case, listening and question-asking skills.

VISUALIZATION TECHNIQUE—TALKING WITH CUSTOMERS

1. Think of the conversation as a gentle flowing river.

2. You and your customer are in one boat; you are steering.

3. Your job is to help the boat stay free from obstructions.

4. You steer with gentle direction.

5. Your goal is to land safely and peacefully at the other end.

6. You never need to use force or too much energy.

7. If the river goes too fast, you are still able to steer the boat safely and keep it under control until you get to calmer water.

8. You have the capability and the energy.

9. You have the strength.

10. You have the will.

Here is a technique you can practice. It is easier with an internal customer or, better still, a close friend or significant other. This is what you do:

- Look into the other person's eyes when he or she is talking to you.
- Do not look away.
- Focus all your attention on the speaker.
- Do not allow your mind to wander.
- When it wanders, bring it back to focus on the other person.
- Listen not just to the words, but to the body language.
- Is the speaker closed (legs, arms) toward you or open?
- Is he fidgeting, scratching his head, or peaceful?
- Is she saying peaceful words but fidgeting?

- Do his words mirror his body language?
- Is she saying how she really feels?
- How can you help the customer express his feelings?
- How can you stop yourself from taking her comments personally?

The last question in that exercise, about *not taking things personally*, is perhaps the hardest component of listening. As soon as we feel threatened or criticized, a huge voice in our head screams at us, "Attack, attack, attack!" This is quickly followed by another huge voice, "Defend, defend, defend!"

If we are not self-aware, we listen to this voice and quickly go from "listening" to "defending" or even "attacking." We will even interrupt the speaker, "Just a minute, that never happened like that. I never said that. It wasn't me." By the time we get defensive, it has become almost impossible for us to offer *Super Service*. The alternative is to get outside our own feelings and focus on the customer's needs.

Understand What a Need Is

To understand the customer's needs, we have to completely rid our mind of what *we think* they want and replace it with what they *really* want.

For example, Cindy knows we want to have our dry cleaning the next day, even though we often don't pick it up until the following week. Is it a headache for her? Sometimes it must be, especially if they are very busy.

Cindy has worked out that we are very good customers. We are loyal, we are regular, we smile, we always pay cash so she doesn't have to bother with credit cards or checks. It's worth her time to give us what we want, which is the comfort of knowing our clothes are clean and available should something unexpected happen, like being called out of town.

Understanding your customer's needs means looking beyond the strict definition of your company's product or service. Here's what to do:

Listen for what they really need/want/desire.

If you're not listening closely, you may provide a basic need, but miss the chance to satisfy a customer's desire! Because the word "desire" is so alien in a book about customer care, we will continue to use the accepted word "need." However, remember that needs represent wants and desires.

Verify and Clarify Needs

One way to check whether you have answered your customer's needs is to clarify the facts. This means restating details, such as numbers, spellings of names and addresses, quantities, timelines, dates, delivery needs, etc.:

- "I understand: There were 15 parts delivered and you needed 25. Is that correct?"

- "Let me see if I understand. You paid the bill on March 1st, and your last statement didn't reflect this?"

- "So, what you're saying, John, is that when the thermostat is on high, it blows out cold air. Have I got it right?"

When you clarify the facts in this way, you are on the way to making sure that all their needs/wants/desires are met. For example, Cindy could say to us, "Five days is too long to wait for the cleaning. You want it next day, correct?" It's a feel-good thing. The customer can breathe a sigh of relief: Aaahh, this person knows what I *really* want.

Barriers to Problem Solving

Some of the barriers to problem solving arise from the *customer's attitude*. For example, the customer:

- Does not want to work with you.
- Wants to work against you.
- Does not trust you.
- Does not respect your ability to help.

The only way to overcome these types of attitudes is to keep your mind focused on the goal: *to help solve their problem*. If you can do this, you will remain unaffected by their attitude. This focus will help you be objective and not take things personally. Remember, to customers you represent your company. You could be a saint, but customers will still regard you with distrust if that is what they have in their mind.

Another barrier to solving problems is *not taking responsibility*. Customers must know that you have taken responsibility for helping them, that you want to correctly diagnose their problem, and that you want to provide the right solution.

In trying to explain the problem, the customer may have difficulty organizing his or her thoughts. You may hear phrases such as:

"It's very confusing … "

"I just can't figure it out … "

"I'm not sure how to … "

"It doesn't seem to … "

Be patient. Remember, you know all about your product; your customer may not. Here are some tips:

1. Speak slowly.

2. Use short sentences.

3. Be tactful.

4. Ask, "Do you have any questions?" or "Am I being clear?"

Most barriers to problems begin and end with people. We must realize that nothing remains the same, that life is about change, and that change brings its own set of problems. Only then can we learn to have a realistic attitude. Then each problem becomes a wonderful opportunity to act in the way we want to be.

Each problem is an opportunity to react as we would expect a peaceful person to react. If we want to become peaceful, it's no good being peaceful all alone on the top of a mountain. The only way to become peaceful is to do so in the middle of a difficult problem.

How we choose to handle problems is up to us, and the beautiful and liberating thing is that we can change. Every moment we have the opportunity to redo our lives. Every moment we can have another go at becoming the person we feel we are inside. The only thing we really need to do is wake up to who we really are!

Honesty as a Tool

If you truly want to help others, you can begin by doing these three things:

1. Think kind thoughts.
2. Speak gently.
3. Use wisdom.

Everything you are inside is reflected in how you treat people. It is almost impossible to think gentle thoughts and act with anger. Alternatively, it is very difficult to think angry thoughts and act with peace. Often our words become a reflection of our ego; they build up the walls around our concept of "me," "mine," "I am a very important person, don't mess with me!"

Begin today to speak the truth. If your product or service has created a problem for your customer, you must acknowledge it. If a customer is distraught about the problem, you must help him or her through it.

Customers have much more faith in a company that is "big" enough to say, "Yes, we made a mistake, and we have enough strength and power behind us to *make good*."

ACTION

It would be a very boring life if we thought of customers as nonbeings, as if they were numbers to "chalk up." We need to personalize our interactions with customers, so that our lives become more interesting and meaningful.

Today and for the rest of your life, do these two things:

1. Become open to listening.

2. Listen for what your customers are feeling, not just for their words.

When you truly listen to others, you will hear "between the lines." You will sense where the words are coming from, rather than just hearing the words. You will feel what others are feeling, and you will be able to respond as a human being responds to a call for help from a child—unselfishly, ready to serve, wanting to be your best.

Chapter 5

CUSTOMER SERVICE KEY 3
COMMUNICATE CLEARLY

We sometimes overwhelm our customer with too much information.
Always think KISS! Keep It Simple and Sincere!

Keep It Simple

We have the power to make our customers feel good or bad just by the way we communicate. Here are a few rules about giving information:

1. **Be clear.** Use simple words without any jargon.
2. **Stick to the point.** Keep focused on the problem and solution.
3. **Be honest.** It's dangerous to overpromise and underperform.

There are also a few phrases to avoid when giving information:

1. **"I'll be honest with you."** This sounds like you haven't been honest until now.
2. **"I can't."** This is like putting a brick wall up between you and your customer. State what you can do, rather than what you can't!
3. **"I'll let you know."** When will you get back? Give a date, a time. Make it happen!

Because information is power, we sometimes overwhelm our customer with too much information. In an attempt to impress, we may use too many technical terms. Keep it simple. Winston Churchill, one of the great communicators of our time, always wrote his speeches for the comprehension level of a 12-year-old. Another master communicator was Benjamin Franklin. He felt voters' rights should not be predicated on ownership of property. His supporters drafted a "white paper" that was overly done and pompous. He told them an easier way: "I own a mule, I can vote. My mule dies, I cannot vote! Therefore the vote represents not me, but my mule!"

Like Ben Franklin, get rid of redundant language. Here are some examples:

Redundant	Use Instead
Assemble together	Assemble
General consensus of opinion	Consensus
Red in color	Red
Basic fundamentals	Fundamentals
Important essentials	Essentials
Due to the fact that	Because
In the event that	If
I am in receipt of	I received

Here are more examples of unnecessary words:

Instead of	Use
We made a recommendation	We recommended
We entered into discussion	We discussed
We made an inspection	We inspected
We performed a study	We studied

There are many ways to speak to be understood; the simplest is to use few words, short words, and short sentences.

Also resist using technical terms and jargon. You probably know all about your product or service and are familiar with the industry jargon. Your company may even have its own language. Because you are so familiar with all these terms, you expect your customers to be. But imagine if doctors had the same expectation. They have every right to; after all, they are dealing with *our bodies*! This equipment carries us around every day; it's our vehicle! We may not know how a VCR works, but our own bodies? Not so! If the doctor talked to us in medical jargon, we might think we had only a couple of months to live: "So my eye infection is caused by all these microorganisms feeding on the *what*?"

Always think KISS: Keep It Simple and Sincere! Here's a technique to help you. On the next page, write down your explanation of how your product or service operates.

PRODUCT/SERVICE PROFILE

Write your explanation of how your product or service operates:

My product/service is called: _____

_____

It works by: _____

_____

Its benefits are: _____

_____

It solves problems by: _____

_____

Other information to add is: _____

_____

_____

Now go back and edit your Product/Service Profile using the following suggestions:

1. **Choose the most familiar words.** If you shouted, "Quick, there's a conflagration!" many people would not know what to do. Why not shout "Fire"?

2. **Eliminate jargon.** Take out any word that looks strange.

3. **Build a foundation of key words.** In school you had to be creative: to say the same thing a different way each time. Outside it is very different: We need to be direct (short and simple is always best).

4. **Trim your sentences.** A long sentence is like nonstop talk. Chop the sentences up to average 15 to 18 words per sentence.

Next time you have to explain your product or service to a customer, use your edited version. It will help you, and it will help them understand what you are talking about.

How to Give Unwelcome Information

We all make mistakes, and sometimes we have to give information that the customer does not want to hear. You must do two things: (1) Accept responsibility, and (2) be direct.

As human beings, we "smell" fear, and it makes us fearful. We see bad news coming and get agitated, so the best way is to get right to the point.

For example, you gave the customer a wrong delivery charge and you cannot adjust it. Using the direct approach, you say, "I'm sorry, I made an error when I quoted the delivery charge. I quoted you $60, and the correct price is $75. I apologize for the mistake and hope it won't cause a problem."

Try to explain the situation in positive rather than negative terms. Which of the following sentences sounds like the person likes the raincoat?

"This raincoat keeps the water out, but it's short."
"This raincoat keeps the water out, and it's short."

The bottom one is much more positive! When we use the word "but," we are eliminating anything good we have said. "This raincoat keeps the water out, *but* ..." means that we don't like the raincoat, even if it does keep the water out.

"This raincoat keeps the water out, *and* ..." means that not only does it keep the water out, but it also has another positive element! Notice when people use the word "but" and listen to what they are really saying. Notice what are you *really* saying when *you* use the word "but."

Good News/Bad News Approach

The good news/bad news approach is an old cliché, and we don't want to say to our customers, "Do you want the good news first, or the bad news?" However, good news/bad news can help in some cases. For example, "To help your situation I've brought the installation forward by two days. However, I apologize for a mistake I made with the delivery charge. The correct price is $75 instead of $60. I'm sorry for the error and any inconvenience."

When we make an error, it's important to accept responsibility for it. If we can sweeten the bad news for the customer, so much the better. That's all!

Encourage the Customer to Participate in Finding the Right Solution

When involved in finding the right solution, the customer is more likely to want the solution to work. Give your customers verbal or nonverbal clues to encourage their participation:

"You mentioned an alternative solution earlier; what did you have in mind?"
"That's interesting. Can you tell me more about that?"

Acknowledge the Customer's Feelings

We can go to a thousand seminars and read a million books about customer care. But until we acknowledge that customers are people and that people have feelings, we may as well throw our money to the wind.

This doesn't mean we must bear the same level of frustration as our customers. Nor does it mean we have to take their frustration on board. All it means is saying with sincerity, "I understand how you must feel, and I apologize. Please tell me what would make it better for you."

Know When to Call in the Manager

At times you have to call in the manager. A manager can bring a new perspective to the situation. A manager can also give the customer more confidence that the problem will be solved.

It is appropriate to call the manager if the customer is very angry, if you have tried every solution possible, and if the customer is still not satisfied. However, even calling in the manager under these circumstances may be admitting defeat too soon. Perhaps you haven't made the customer feel that you really care or have the authority to solve the problem. In other words, you don't trust yourself, and the customer doesn't trust you!

Absolutely call in the manager when you haven't got the authority to provide the solution, or when you have explored every solution and there is nothing left. Remember, though, that calling in the manager is a very last resort. Why? In this case, you think you lack the power to resolve the problem and really you don't! If it were your own business and this were your very best customer, you would resolve the problem yourself; always look for every possible solution before you turn to the manager for help.

CHECK-IN

Write down the top three problems your customers encounter:

1. _____

2. _____

3. _____

Now write down the solutions and pin them up so you know how to answer them next time the problem occurs:

1. _____

2. _____

3. _____

Chapter 6

CUSTOMER SERVICE KEY 4
REACH AGREEMENT

Incorporate the customer's ideas into your solution.

To reach agreement, we must be of one mind with the customer. How? We suspend our own agenda and listen.

Working with Diversity, Not against It

Some people are afraid to listen to others, as if listening means agreeing with everything that's being said. But listening doesn't mean agreeing. Every summer, an elderly parent comes to stay with us for a couple of months. Often during that time, we hear very strong opinions that would definitely be grounds for dismissal at most "politically correct" workplaces. Who are we to judge? We didn't live through World War II, weren't separated from our spouse by war, and haven't had to send dead rabbits home through the mail for the hungry family subsisting on food rations.

Each person's history makes it seem as though we all live on different planets. How do we become of one mind and in agreement about anything? The answer: We do so with wisdom, compassion, and a desire to reach agreement.

Wanting to reach agreement means we want it more than we want combat. We want harmony more than we want arguments. Again, it doesn't mean we lie down and take whatever the customer wants to throw at us. It simply means we want agreement.

For example, with elderly parents, our focus is to provide a comfortable, safe, and loving environment—to include them in everything we do, places we go, friends we see. The result is a harmonious experience for all of us. Sometimes we say in a playful tone, "Wow, is that what you really believe?" or, "I don't think that's a good thing to repeat in company." Mainly, we listen to the wisdom, the stories, the commonsense approach to life.

It's no different from being with a customer who has outdated opinions. "I can see why you feel that way, and another way to look at it is … ." Or, "If this is a recurring problem, maybe we should explore the whole scenario."

Looking for the Win-Win Solution

Of course, there are always customers who are looking for a freebie—who try to get a replacement product, even when they have obviously been abusing the original. How you deal with that depends on:

- Company policy
- Whether the customer needs training on product use
- The costs involved (actual cost, goodwill)

Your customers may really believe they are not doing anything wrong with the product or service. It just isn't working!

Super Service is about seeking harmony and balance with your customers. Reaching agreement is not a battle of power. Many of us are raised to be competitive, to fight, to win, and to be first. We've all heard the coach state, "Winning is not the most important thing; it's the only thing!"

We all have this impulse to win; the problem is that if the customer wins, you lose. Or if you win, the customer loses.

If we turn these competitive urges into complementary urges, we all get what we need. The inner battles stop. The conflict stops. The *selfish* chatter of "me, me, me" stops. Reaching agreement is making it right for everyone concerned. The statement, "Do unto others as you would have them do unto you," becomes a living action, and your heart figuratively opens.

But we're not advocating giving away the whole shop. This is a business book, and the most profitable business is a direct result of *Super Service*. Do you know the costs involved in your solutions? You should! *Super Service* is about reaching agreements in the most profitable way. Can you answer the following questions?

1. How much does your product/service cost to repair?
2. How much does your product/service cost to replace?
3. How important are customers to your company?
4. Do certain customers deserve special treatment?
5. How loyal are your customers?

As a service provider trying to solve customer problems, you need to be looking for the least expensive ways to satisfy your customers. Your job is to help your company make a profit and to do it in the most harmonious way for all concerned. Sometimes serving a customer profitably is not possible and we have to turn away the business.

We once decided that we did not want to do business with a particular customer. Why? We had done one project a year for the past two years, we had never made a profit, and the job always turned out to be a nightmare. From the get-go, we were "nickel-and-dimed" to death. There was no profit margin, and the aggravation for our staff was too much for the job to be worthwhile. The projects took a lot of energy, the person in charge was very difficult to deal with, and—bottom line—we had to wait over five months for our invoice to be paid. Sometimes it is better to walk away from "bad" business than to be depleted of energy and profit.

We hope we have made it clear that *Super Service* is not about throwing ourselves at the feet of every customer. We are not promoting the subservient characters out of Charles Dickens, tugging on our forelock with cap in hand!

How to Seek Win-Win Solutions

There are many books about negotiating. We ask that you move beyond the accepted concept and place your mind at a higher level—we could even say a more enlightened level. *Super Service* is about achieving harmony by becoming totally straightforward and honest with ourselves. We strive to purify our thoughts and attitudes and create a working environment that promotes openness, kindness, and wise communication. This objective is hard to achieve if we are thinking of negotiation tactics and countertactics.

How about turning the negotiating concept inside out and upside down? What about listening to what customers really need and want? What about suspending our own judgments and treating customers (who may be strangers or even people you dislike) as if they are beloved relatives who have a serious problem? Imagine customers are beloved relatives. How would you help them?

You would probably want them to be happy, satisfied, content. You would *really* listen to the issues and want to help resolve them. If they had a grievance, you would actually understand why they are hurting. You would show compassion and empathy because they are close to you. Why not treat your customers this way?

Try it tomorrow at work. Empty your mind and be everything you can be for the other person. And don't worry that your mind will remain empty; as soon as the person stops talking, your mind will be as full as ever! And when the customer has gone, you will start talking to yourself again as usual!

"Did I really empty my mind for him?"

"Did I have the desire to serve like the book said?"

"Was I judgmental?"

"Was I sincere about his problem?"

Build on the Customer's Proposal

Have you ever been in a conversation that seems to flow beautifully and you don't know why? It's often because that person is mirroring something that we like in ourselves. It is the same when we listen to a speaker. If he or she is saying something that we agree with, we nod our heads in agreement, as if we are the ones up there saying it!

When customers propose something, it's not a good idea to say, "No, we have to do it this way." Instead, we should build on their proposal. Here are some guidelines:

Build on the Customer's Proposal

1. Explain to the customer why you offered the solution and how it will help the situation.

2. Ask questions to gain a better understanding of the situation.

3. Check your understanding by explaining the problem in your own words.

4. Incorporate the customer's ideas into your solution.

5. Build and communicate on the joint ideas.

Be Creative

We all have huge amounts of creativity; some people are more open to using it than others. Creativity means being open to new ideas. Sometimes, we think that creativity in business is different from creativity in the artist's studio. Not so. Creativity is creativity wherever it is applied.

If you get into a slump, it becomes visible to everyone around you; be creative in finding your way out, and ask yourself the following questions:

1. What worked in the past?
2. What is not working now?
3. What can I do differently?
4. What resources do I have?

Have fun getting out of your rut:

1. Dress differently for a day. (It doesn't need to be drastic. For example, if you normally wear black, wear red.)
2. Style your hair differently and see how it makes you feel.
3. Find a good joke to tell everyone.
4. Eat different food from what you would normally choose.
5. Cut out the coffee and find a new way to wake up.

Promises

Don't overpromise and underperform. If you give a false set of expectations for yourself or your company, you may not be able to meet them down the road. It is misleading to:

1. Give the impression that the product will be repaired at no cost, if in fact that is not the truth.
2. Allow customers to think their equipment will be repaired much sooner than is possible, just to calm them down.

Here are some ways to calm customers down, without misleading them or overpromising:

1. "You do not have coverage for this repair. I can provide a service contract that will take only two days to put through and will benefit you for one year. The cost for that is $_____. May I do this for you?"

2. "Ms. Jones, I cannot schedule the service call until Wednesday morning. There are no time slots until then. However, I am putting you down for first priority if there is a cancellation. How does that sound?"

3. "I certainly understand why you need a copy of the invoice today, Mr. Smith; unfortunately, the report doesn't come out until tomorrow. I will get the request in right away to be processed first, so I can call you by 10 o'clock tomorrow morning. Will that be satisfactory?"

How to Not Give away the Shop

Here's something to keep in mind: *You do not have to do whatever the customer suggests.*

Here are two questions that will help you make the right decision:

1. Does the customer's proposal truly answer his or her needs?

2. Will it satisfy and resolve the issue?

The best proposal is the one that keeps both parties in business.

Sometimes the customer's proposal is overly demanding. Since we want to have *Super Service*, however, we should never tell customers they are being unreasonable—or should we? If you bottle up resentment and anger you will feel ill. Imagine if you had a bottle labeled "ANGER!" You would not want to swallow it. Dealing with anger or resentment means releasing it as you experience it, moment by moment. However, this statement is not intended to give you carte blanche to spill your emotions all over your customers.

Frustration and anger are emotions that flare up when we feel challenged. We become like knights of old: Our shield comes up and our words act like spears. We would be better to act like Star Trek—shields up, assess the situation without the spears.

Here are some suggestions on how to not give away the shop, and yet still honor your own feelings. One is to use humor.

The customer says, "I want a new product. This one doesn't work; you have to replace it today!"

With a hint of laughter in your voice, say, "I agree, after three years it probably does need replacing! However, we can probably service it and replace some of the parts for a much lower cost!"

This way, you've let the customer know that whatever happens, it's going to cost something to replace an old product that's gone way past its warranty date. You're looking at the customer as if you are standing side by side on the same side of the fence instead of on opposite sides feeling ill will toward each other.

You can exceed customer expectations without giving something away: Ask an extra question, give an extra smile, or respond to the problem promptly.

CHECK-IN

The task is to use phrases that show the customer your "good heart." We're talking about open-hearted wisdom. Here's the clue: Since every action is preceded by a thought, we have to think good thoughts before we speak. Here are a few examples:

Think: **We are on the same side of the fence.**

Say: "I like your idea about …"

Think: **We want the same thing.**

Say: "We can work with your suggestion to …"

Think: **I want the best for both.**

Say: "From my experience I think your best option is …"

Think: **One small step is all it takes.**

Say: "I like your idea, and perhaps we can also …"

ACTION

After you have had some practice thinking good thoughts, you are now ready to speak. In your upcoming interactions with customers, speak from a place of good intention.

Note: Difficulties don't disappear, they are a part of life, especially in customer care. How we react to the difficulties makes the difference. Think good thoughts. Speak with wisdom and you will make the difference.

1. Choose one of the examples from the check-in on the previous page.

2. Copy the example in bold red pen on a piece of 8½×11-inch paper.

3. Pin the paper where you can see it.

4. Refer to it throughout the day as a reminder.

Chapter 7

CUSTOMER SERVICE KEY 5
CHECK UNDERSTANDING

When you explain to customers *how* their service need will be met by your organization, they feel in control.

Checking understanding with your customers gives them an opportunity to confirm that your solution meets their needs. It *does not mean restating the problem*. It means restating the steps of the solution in terms of cost, time, service steps, etc.

Here are the steps:

1. Make sure the customers understand the solution you've offered them.

2. Be prepared for customer input.

3. Verify the facts.

4. Check for agreement of plan.

5. Accept responsibility.

6. End on a positive note.

Unfortunately, these steps don't always go easily.

What the Customer Needs to Know

She's a man-hater! This was a problem that came up during a brainstorming session with a group of high-tech service providers. They wanted help with a customer: "She doesn't want help! She won't give us access to the users! We can't implement the development stage. She's a control freak! She's chemically imbalanced!" The problem had become very personal, and the service providers were now highly charged and emotional.

We brainstormed the solutions: communicate, educate, help, get sign-off to continue, run away, hand off, bypass, and so on. But they kept going back to the problems—even when we had moved on to the solutions. They had lost all objectivity. The customer had become such a nightmare, they *wanted* to "lose her!"

"We're halfway through. We've made a good profit so far; we could hand it off to another group to finish!"

What had gone so wrong that it had come to this? When we talked about it further, we discovered that they had not *understood the customer's needs*. Their customer had been "burned" a couple of times in the recent past, and our service providers didn't realize that her experience had affected her responses. They had not addressed what their customer needed to know:

1. **Time:** How long was the project going to take?
2. **Target:** What will the outcome look like?
3. **Budget:** How much will it cost?
4. **Benefit:** Why are we doing the project?

Without a well-stated goal and without "checking understanding," our service providers were having a difficult time going back to their customer and saying, "This is what we said we would do, in this amount of time, for this amount of money, for this benefit. We're now here. We've spent this amount, and we're nowhere near completion."

For a large project with your customer, you must have a well-defined goal and sign-off. Then, when the customer wants changes, you can say with hand on heart, "Sure we can do that; let's take a look at how that will impact the budget and deadline of the project."

In our brainstorming session, our customer service providers decided to talk to their customer about the project plan and, if possible, redefine the goals and tasks. By concentrating on the project plan, they would return objectivity to the situation. They could start working together with their customer instead of waging war.

Other service providers in this workshop talked about how one of their customers didn't want to pay the invoice. "They say we haven't done enough work to justify our costs!" This is another good reason for putting together a project plan and writing down all the tasks, subtasks, and even sub-subtasks. We need to see what we're getting for our money, and customers typically don't know all the work that goes into a product or a service.

Do you? Are you fully aware of all the tasks that you perform? Often we are so used to doing our job, we are unaware of how much time it takes to do certain tasks.

Tasks = Time = Money

After you have written a goal for a large project, brainstorm with a colleague all the tasks necessary to bring it to completion. Itemizing the tasks helps your customer understand the size of the project and also where the money is going.

Customers' needs are not hard to understand. What do you want? What do your customers want? Underneath everything, we all want the same things: security, love, and human kindness. We all want to feel we made a good deal, that we didn't get "screwed." We need to know that if we paid money for something, it will work and, if it doesn't work, it gets replaced (as long as we haven't abused it and it is still under warranty!).

Standard Operating Procedure (SOP)

You, me, your customers, your boss, your peers, and your colleagues all have standard operating procedures—the habits we have learned. The problem is we're usually too asleep to notice that we are using them.

What is your standard operating procedure? How do you react when the chips are down? Are you a giver or a taker?

You've probably heard of the fight-or-flight syndrome. If we get into trouble, either we stand and fight or we flee. Do you know what your reaction is? Become aware of it. Do you like an argument? Do you enjoy a battle? Or do you walk away? Drive off? Steer clear?

Learning how to handle your own problems will help you to understand other people's problems because you will recognize them. There are four stages to this learning:

1. Awareness.
2. Awkwardness.
3. Skill.
4. Habit.

First we become **aware** that we need or want to learn something different. Let's say that our standard operating procedure when dealing with customers is to be very judgmental. The first step is to know and recognize that we are judgmental.

You will know if you have this trait by just one thing: When you first meet customers, do you judge their clothes, how they speak, how they hold themselves, etc.? Or do you let all appearances fall away and see them simply as human beings?

The second stage in learning is **awkwardness.** This occurs, for example, when you become aware of being judgmental and you decide not to be. Changing will be very awkward for you at first. Your SOP will want to put your customer into a "box," because that seems easier to deal with.

As another example, if your standard operating procedure is to gossip and you have become aware of it, go through the awkward stage of not being a gossip. Zip your mouth.

This takes you to the third stage: **skill.** It takes skill not to be a gossip! It means that you have to be in the present moment. If you enjoy what is happening right now—this very moment—you will come to realize there is no point in gossiping or being judgmental. There is no good in any of the other standard operating procedures that your mind has programmed for you.

This brings us to the fourth stage of learning: turning a new skill into a **habit.** Don't fall asleep and let yourself go to default. Listen to yourself, be aware of what you are saying and what action you are taking. Eventually, you will form the habit of being awake in your life. This is an important concept— to be awake. Where is your true self? We all have the same needs and wants and urges. Follow someone who is awake and don't be concerned about people liking you all the time. Do and say what you know is right.

Make your life something wonderful. Take time with people. If you are given a rotten job to do, do it as well as you can. Become a shining example for yourself and others. Light up your world! Light up your customers!

Manage Customer Expectations

Tell your customers what to expect. If we know what is going to happen, we feel in control. When we don't know what is going to happen, we feel as though we are in a luge competition, hurtling down and around at a high speed without an end in sight.

If your plan is to hand over the customer's problem to the billing department, be sure to tell the customer and the billing department. Tell customers they don't have to re-explain everything, that you have done it for them, and that they should contact you again if they experience any problems.

If the customer's problem means bringing in a third party or even another company, explain the "why-when-how."

However, as we have said before, you don't want to give away the entire shop. You are part of a business. Your job is to help your company grow profitably. Look at the two words: profit and loss! "Profit" has a glow to it, a life. "Loss" is something to be bereaved. You want to be profitable and to do so for the best of all concerned.

If you can help make your customers profitable, you are providing a wonderful service. Take a moment to write a list of everything about your product or service that will help your customer be profitable. Think in terms of saving them time or money, although the profitability can be in the "feel-good" or reaching-a-goal department.

I HELP MY CUSTOMERS BE PROFITABLE BY:

1. _____

2. _____

3. _____

4. _____

Being *with* the Customer

Are you *with* the customers when you are with them? We often "brush" people off just because they don't fit into our image. That sounds harsh, doesn't it? Yet every time we dismiss people without finding out who they are, we are saying that they may as well not exist.

We all have a list of people whom we want to dismiss. Some think the elderly have nothing to offer. Others may think children are too noisy or that teenagers are undisciplined. The list goes on and on.

Be more self-aware and start living! *Super Service* never stops! It's there with you all the time—in and out of the office, at the department store, at the agency, in the salon, wherever it is that you work. *Super Service* is not something you can turn on and off whimsically.

We're not saying that you have to spend all your time listening to a customer's personal problems or doing everything for one particular customer. Being with a customer means simply being present to help if we can, to extend a helping hand when we can, to light up somebody's world with a smile.

Does this sound too simple—as if this is not about your job? Do you think your work is so stressful that you don't have time for the "people stuff"? The problem is that people are everything. We are social animals, in case you hadn't noticed.

In one of our project management courses, we discussed PERT charts, GANTT charts, work breakdown structures, crash path analysis, and task analysis worksheets. In the end, however, the most difficult thing to analyze was the people.

Yet it's so simple. We all have needs. We all have the same needs. Therefore personalize your service. Pledge to help. Be honest. Be open to new information from your customer. Even when you have an action plan in mind, and after you have reached agreement about how the problem should be solved, your customer may still have input. Be prepared to listen. Maintain the desire to serve.

Who is the most important person to you? *You* are! Customers are no different. They are the most important people to themselves. *Super Service* requires that you become *no thing* so that you can become *every thing* for your customer.

PHRASES TO AVOID

"I can."

"I can."

"I can."

"I can."

If you say "I can," the other person will think "Yes, but will you?" We tend to put up a lot of smokescreens when we talk to customers:

"I think I can do that!"

"If I get this by tomorrow, I can probably do that!"

"I can do that if you do this!"

These phrases do not inspire confidence. They do not tell the customer, "It will be done!"

PHRASES TO USE

"I will."

"I will."

"I will."

"I will."

When we say "We will," we are saying that something will be done. Now comes the integrity part: Do you do what you say you are going to do? Or not? Do you sometimes do what you say if you feel in the right mood?

If you say you will do something for your customer, you must do it! If you do not think you can do something, you must say that you cannot do it! If you say you will try to do something, you are saying that it probably won't happen.

"I will send your request to ..."

"I will talk to my manager ..."

"I will get a service engineer out tomorrow ..."

"I will take this to accounts payable ..."

Become a person of integrity. Do what you say you will do.

CHECK-IN

Pin up this checklist where you can see it to remind you of the steps involved in checking understanding.

1. **Make sure the customer understands what you intend to do:** "So, to clarify, for the next three days the service engineer will come. Is this correct?"

2. **Be prepared for customer input.**

3. **Check notes:** This is your last chance to verify facts.

4. **Check for agreement of plan:** "Will these steps meet your needs?"

5. **Accept responsibility:** "Call me if there are any further issues."

6. **End on a positive note:** "I'm glad it worked out."

ACTION

Use your check-in list with the six steps during the next week. Work on checking understanding with all your customers. For one morning only, ask yourself the following questions:

1. Did I use the steps with my customers?

2. Do my customers understand how much my product/service/repair is going to cost, and how long it will take?

3. Am I giving my customers the understanding they need?

Obtaining customer understanding is much easier before the event than after.

Chapter 8

CUSTOMER SERVICE KEY 6
TAKE ACTION

Taking action not only helps you and the person you are helping.
It leads you to enlightenment.

Actions speak louder than words. We all know the people in our lives whom we can depend on and those we cannot—who keeps their word and who doesn't. The strange thing is that often the people who don't keep their word speak longer and louder than those who do!

Have you noticed how some people jump into projects only to get burned out halfway through? It's easy to do and there are many reasons:

1. **Boredom:** The project loses its sparkle.
2. **Complexity:** It's harder than we thought.
3. **Resources:** We haven't got the people or equipment.
4. **Money:** We've run out of cash.
5. **Time:** It's taking too long.

You can probably come up with a lot more reasons why projects don't get finished.

However, there is a simple remedy—so simple you may not want to hear it. Here it is: *Don't start something you can't finish!*

What does that mean? It means take a look at your life. How do you manage it? Do you have too many things on your plate at once? If so, delegate or finish what you have before taking on anything else. If your boss asks you to take on more, say, "Does this take priority over projects 3, 4, and 5? Or do you want me to finish those first?"

Pointing out that you have other things that need doing is not rude. It is rude if you say it in a nasty or a harassed way.

Turning Negatives into Positives

Are you using too many negative words? Do you hear yourself saying every day, "I'm tired," "I can't do this," "I hate this," or "I'm bored!"? Maybe you need to change the CD.

The beliefs you have about yourself are extremely powerful because they become what other people see in you. If you go around moaning, that's what people hear. Your chant makes you the person you are!

Think about the unhappy people in your life. What words do they use? If you close your eyes for a moment and visualize their faces in front of you, they probably look sad and, if you listen carefully, you will hear them repeating over and over their sad words.

If you're like that, what can you do? First you have to be aware! What do you say? How do you say it? Listen to the words that seem to pop out of your mouth without your even knowing. Then comes the awkward phase. When you hear the words pop out, you have to say the opposite. If you say, "I'm bored," say instead, "That's not really true, I'm really very content!"

We hope that you don't use negative words with your customers. (Remember: "My customer is anyone who is not me!" (Whomever you are talking with is your customer. Your words are like seeds; they scatter and fall all over your world. People hear them and learn what kind of person you are. Change your words and you will change your life. Instead of "I can't do numbers," say "I'm getting better at numbers!" In the following list, pick out one or two negative phrases that you recognize yourself as saying. Start using the positive affirmations instead:

Instead of ...	Use ...
"I hate myself."	"I love myself."
"I'm bored."	"I'm content!"
"It'll never happen."	"It will happen!"
"Nothing works out for me."	"Everything works out for me!"
"I never get what I want."	"I get everything I want!"
"My life is horrible."	"My life is great!"
"My customers are all difficult."	"My customers are all great!"
"I can't find happiness."	"I have happiness!"
"I'm not fulfilled."	"I am fulfilled."

It cannot be stressed enough that thought precedes action. *Super Service* recommends that you become aware of your thoughts. If you have lots of negative thoughts, get rid of them by writing them down and then burning the paper (these are not meant to be seen by others). Then take action in something positive.

Here's an example. Some of us wake up in the morning feeling depressed. We don't know why; it just seems to happen, except we are in charge of our thoughts. What you think of as a horrible prospect—of another workday—can now become your greatest gift! You have the opportunity to change for the better! Replace a depressing thought with a good one. "I hate my customers" becomes "I am going to do a great job for them!" "I hate my job" becomes "I am going to learn everything I can in this job!"

If you change your thinking, you will change your actions.

Gandhi said, "How I live my life, that is my teaching." We are the same. If we profess peace in public and kick the cat in private, we are not fooling anyone but ourselves. If we then beat ourselves up because we kicked the cat, we are even trying to fool ourselves, but it won't work.

Right Thought Comes before Right Action

Your customers want you to take action on their behalf. They come to you because they have nowhere else to go. If they could solve the problem themselves, they would. Think about your own experience as a customer. It takes time and effort to make a complaint or return defective merchandise. Most of us don't want the hassle. But think about the time when a service provider helped you—when you got more than you even imagined! Wasn't it fabulous? Didn't it restore your faith in human beings?

Why not be that person yourself? Why not restore faith in humankind? When you say you are going to take action, don't pass the buck; instead, make it happen! Become known as a person who gets the job done. And when you can't do a job, you say with hand on heart, "I can't do this right now. When I have some free time I will!"

Taking action not only helps you and the person you are helping, it leads you to enlightenment. You feel a purity, a knowledge that you are pure and that your heart is open.

When you take the right action, you wipe your internal slate clean from past mistakes. Your internal state of being feels cleaner, purer, more blissful. Think about the number of drug addicts who turned their lives around to help others. They could do that only because they understand the pain, suffering, and how to help.

You have the choice. You can choose to beat yourself up or change your thoughts and take right action. The "process" of your life makes you the person you are. The process through which you help your customers determines whether they are happy or not.

As an example, in an ice cream parlor yesterday, we were served by someone who, in the words of the friend who was with us, "made the hair on my neck stand on end!" Of course we made allowances. "Maybe he lost his mother!" "Maybe he has money problems." Yet the ice cream took on the flavor of the server. It didn't taste as good or as sweet as it could have. The grumpy demeanor of the server "poisoned" the ice cream!

We can do the same with our customers without even knowing it. We can go through the process exactly right: Use the right phrases, say the right things, produce the right solution, and ask at the end, "Is everything okay?"

Customers might reply, "Ah, yes, everything's great, thank you!" Yet, as they walk away, they're thinking, "I'm never going to use that place again!" The grumpy demeanor is what people remember. We can try to cover it up with words later on, but it doesn't really help. The problem is that customers don't want to hear excuses. They want us to take the right action and, if we take the wrong action, they never forget.

In our lives, we can remarry the same person over and over again, go for the same kind of job over and over, find ourselves repeatedly in the same troubled situations. All the while we wonder, "How on earth did this happen again!"

The reason: We forget! We forget the consequences from the last time we did that action. We forget that the last time we spoke to people that way, they got mad. Ultimately, we don't want to clearly see ourselves, because we are too fearful of what we might find! Yet we take a clear look at ourselves, we are not nearly as bad as we think we are—and we can change!

Change is a strange thing. You may have heard the phrase, "A leopard can't change its spots." However, it seems to be a different thing when we are talking about a caterpillar. Caterpillars do change. They transform into butterflies.

Do we as human beings have the capacity to change? Absolutely and without a doubt! Just look around. You know people who have changed: alcoholics who have been on the wagon for decades, drug addicts who have reformed their lives, and on and on.

If you want to become the kind of person who can be relied on, who will complete tasks and be committed, you must first have the right thought: "I commit myself to this task and will see it through completion with a joy-filled heart!"

Is that too much for you? Then take out some of the words and just say, "I commit myself to a joy-filled heart!"

Behavior Is What Customers Remember

If you have listened to your customers and identified their needs, you are ready to carry out the action plan. This means taking action to ensure that the right steps are taken, by the right people, as fast as possible. Simply stated: It means doing what you said you would do!

You need to follow up with your customers, keeping them informed of any progress or delays. Many customers complain about a lack (particularly in large organizations) of communication between departments or employees. To reduce this cause of friction, make sure you let the right people know what they need to know. Keeping people informed before something happens is much easier than telling them after the event.

Often, the small tasks that we put off create the most problems, like answering our messages. We're tired; we don't want to return calls. We put things off until later, but it doesn't get any easier; it just gets later! So our suggestion is:

1. Act on messages as soon as you get them.
2. Respond to your voice/e-mail as soon as you receive it.
3. Put things back where you found them.
4. Keep people informed of any changes that affect them.

On the next page are six keys to taking action the right way. Incidentally, when you write your e-mail in all capital letters, it looks as though you are shouting. Also, keep follow-up guidelines short, simple, and to the point.

TAKE ACTION

1. **Give regular updates and progress reports.** Let customers know what is going on so they are prepared.

2. **Communicate delays promptly.** If customers know about delays, they can make changes in their schedules.

3. **State exactly what was done.** Without using technical terms or jargon, explain what was done and what steps you have taken.

4. **Give a personal reassurance to the customer.** Tell the customer that you have solved the problem.

5. **Help your customer to be proactive.** By providing information about preventive maintenance, you help yourself and your customer.

6. **Thank your customer.** As always, the customer has made an effort to bring the issue to your attention. It is much better to be told something is not working than for the customer to switch to the competition.

When the Company Is Used as an Excuse for Bad Action

Sometimes, it seems easy to blame the company for the problem:

"Oh, those people in service, they never do things on time!"

"I wish they'd get their act together in accounting!"

"We've had lots of similar problems in the past."

When customers hear phrases like these, what are they to think?

"This person has no loyalty to the company. It mustn't be such a great company if they hire people who talk this way!"

"I have no confidence in this person or the company."

"I'm glad this person doesn't work for me!"

When we moved offices, we had to have new phones installed. The engineers didn't arrive when they were supposed to. We called and were told it would be six days before they could come out. Meanwhile, we were supposed to function without phones! We got them to come out two days later.

When the engineer came, he said, "I only put the lines in, I'm not supposed to touch the phones!" The new phones came with a 60-page booklet! We needed help to understand how to transfer calls, page other offices, etc. Finally, when the engineer realized the task ahead, he started to get mad—not at us, but at his phone company. "I don't think those people in the office know what they're doing!" he said. "I think the sales person sold you *too much phone*! Do you really need all these functions?"

His reaction made us uncomfortable. Had we bought a phone system that was too sophisticated for our needs? Could we rely on this person to do a good job?

Bad-mouthing your company is a lose-lose situation. If what you say is true, then do something about it. Talk to the people in accounting, service, or wherever the problem is. It's up to you to take pride in where you work.

We complained to the phone company and got the installation charge taken off. We felt somewhat better, but we would still have preferred it not to have happened in the first place. Why?

1. We were out of contact with our customers for two days.

2. It was a hassle to solve the problem.

3. We had to lodge a complaint, which takes time and energy.

What happened next was also not good. When we got our bill, the installation charge had not been taken off. It took almost an entire day to track down the right person to take the charge off the bill. It took another amount of effort to explain what happened. It was a disaster in customer service follow-up.

On the next page are some guidelines that would help eliminate what happened to us.

GUIDELINES FOR FOLLOW-UP

1. **Confirm that the problem is resolved.** Once a problem is solved, the customer may not know it's been solved. Use phrases like, "I've taken care of the installation charge. It will not appear on your next statement. If you have any questions please call [*your name, phone number or reference number*] as a contact."

2. **Verify satisfaction.** Find out if the solution meets the customer's needs and be prepared to accept a positive or negative response. For example, you could say, "I'm calling to follow up and make sure your invoice is correct. I hope your phone system is working well for you now."

   Do not show disappointment or frustration if the customer says "no!" Keep your tone of voice steady and calm and find out what is wrong.

3. **Check for new problems and/or opportunities.** Sometimes, one solution brings up other problems or opportunities to do more business. So never be afraid to find out what is happening and how the customer feels.

As usual, there are phrases to use and phrases to avoid. Generally, they are fairly commonsense ones.

PHRASES TO AVOID

"It's usually an operator problem and not the product."

"I don't understand why you are still frustrated. I thought the problem was solved!"

"Have they been able to sort out your problem yet?"

PHRASES TO USE

"Let me make sure I have the right number: 6587, is that correct?"

"I'm adding your name to our database, so we can contact you when our new enhancements come out. Is that okay?"

"It was a pleasure working with you, and thank you for bringing your problem to our attention."

"Your account has been credited."

"Your system is now working correctly."

"Does this meet your needs?"

CHECK-IN

Think about all the ways you can improve on taking action. Add your personal take-action steps at the end of the following list:

1. Take initiative.
2. Be responsible.
3. Be willing to make decisions.
4. Use right thinking before acting.
5. Get input from customer.
6. Listen for clues as to how the customer is feeling.
7. Develop a clear mental picture of the situation.
8. Use compassion when speaking the truth.
9. Remember we all want the same things.
10. Keep your tone quiet and peaceful.
11. Let your barriers down.
12. Have a desire to serve.
13. Clarify, verify, and check for mutual agreement on problems.
14. Communicate delays promptly.
15. Explain the action plan steps.
16. Reassure the customer that the solution has been accomplished.
17. Thank the customer.
18. Get the action plan done within the stated time frame.
19. Find other potential requirements.
20. _____
21. _____
22. _____
23. _____
24. _____

ACTION

On your next customer interaction, ask yourself the following question: How can I improve my follow-up actions so that I complete things in a responsible way?

- Once you have answered this question, you have moved into awareness.

- The next step is to push through awkwardness. In other words, it will feel awkward to bring new follow-up actions into your work routine until you feel comfortable with the skill.

- Keep using the skill until it becomes a habit. This is when you do the step without thinking. This is when you can pat yourself of the back and say, "I did it!"

Chapter 9

CUSTOMER SERVICE KEY 7
BUILD ON SATISFACTION

Added value means going the extra mile or beyond the call of duty.

A psychiatrist friend once told us, "When clients come to me for self-improvement or counseling on a problem, I always ask them to tell me about a time when everything 'worked' really well for them. Then we build on that." It's the same with customers. Yes, we have to listen to the problem, but do we ever think to build on their satisfactions? Do we think to ask questions like:

"When it worked well, what was the best aspect?"

"Can you tell me about the best part of the product or service, and how that worked for you?"

One of the hardest parts about delivering *Super Service* is that we always focus on the problem; but what if the perceived customer problem isn't really the problem? What if the product wasn't working well for the customer even when it was working?

For example, a telephone system designed for three phone outlets will be frustrating if there are five people in the office wanting to use the phone at the same time. If the customer calls with a problem on one of the telephones and it is fixed, it still doesn't solve the overall problem that there aren't enough units to handle the calls. Suppose you ask, "How did the system handle your needs when everything was working well?" You might get the response, "It was never any good!" Then you need to probe more. "What was the reason for buying the product?"

When you are building on satisfaction, be sure to emphasize that you will work with customers to find a solution and that you want to make sure the solution will work well for them into the future.

Be Helpful

Keep your customer informed of new and helpful data. In this high-tech world, products and services change daily. If software companies waited to release their product only when it had the final upgrade or enhancement, the product would never make the stores.

Correspondingly, customers could wait forever to buy the final software versions. So, as a *Super Service* provider, you can keep customers informed of new product enhancements and services. Here's an example:

"Just for your information, would you like to hear about the new enhancement for your system 300? I think it will help reduce the problems you've been experiencing."

On the Front Line

Make your job your business. It makes no sense to be a *Super Service* provider if you don't take your job seriously.

Think of yourself as a business owner. After all, you are at the front line, liaising between the customer and your company. Take responsibility for your job and your customers. If you are waiting for the computer to access customer account information, ask the customer if he or she has been satisfied with prior orders. This may uncover "opportunities" to provide and sell additional services. No matter how good the product, if the service provider isn't doing a good job, the customer will not stick around, especially if competition is selling the same type of product or service.

Besides helping your company be successful, you get the feeling of achievement. If you lose this job, your skills are easily transferable because you are a valuable asset to any company.

And before we hear trumpets heralding, what about plain and simple added value?

Added value means going the extra mile or beyond the call of duty. It means giving a free service call if the customer has lost business because of a company error. It means going beyond the customer's expectations by being aware of how you can exceed them without extra cost to your company.

CHECK-IN

Think back to yesterday and list your successes. List everything and anything: from not eating the chocolate donut, to helping a colleague find a document, to staying late to finish a project, to getting home early because it was your child's birthday.

Make the list of all your successes in the following spaces:

1. _____
2. _____
3. _____
4. _____
5. _____
6. _____
7. _____
8. _____
9. _____
10. _____
11. _____
12. _____
13. _____
14. _____
15. _____
16. _____
17. _____

ACTION

Build on your successes. We all know and constantly beat ourselves up about our unsuccessful stuff. Now it's time to turn yourself inside out and see the good parts of yourself. Follow these steps:

1. Tomorrow, when you wake up in the morning, repeat to yourself, "Today I will build on my successes!"

2. Take just one of the successful actions that you listed, and build on it today. Each day pick a different one.

3. Know that by taking this action, you will move forward into recognizing that you are a successful person! You accomplish successful things in your life. You are awake to your successes and you build on them.

Part III
ADVANCED CUSTOMER SERVICE SKILLS

Chapter 10

HOW TO HANDLE AN UNHAPPY CUSTOMER

It doesn't matter if customers are right or wrong.
They need to air their complaint.

Customers fall into two main emotional categories: happy and unhappy. The happy customer is friendly and calm. The unhappy customer is frustrated and angry. If you were to think of customers in terms of traffic lights, here's how they would look:

Happy	=	Green	=	Go
Neutral	=	Yellow	=	Caution
Unhappy	=	Red	=	Stop

Creating Unhappy Customers

This chapter deals mainly with how to handle unhappy customers. However, it is important to know that happy customers can easily be triggered into becoming unhappy. For example, being put on hold too long or a misinterpreted tone of voice can trigger a change in their emotional state.

Let's explore how a happy customer turns into an unhappy one: The customer calls to check her account status. You may have just handled a very difficult customer and are still feeling the effects. You have tension in your voice. Suddenly the seemingly happy customer says,

"Do you talk to all your customers in that tone of voice? I might not be your biggest customer, but I've been using your company for ten years now. I expect better treatment."

Or you put the customer on hold to gather some information; you realize it's gone beyond the acceptable 30 seconds but feel he will not mind. When you get him back on the phone, he says,

"I've been on hold for ages. I just called to check on my account, but you obviously don't care about my time ... ."

Or the customer expects to have the installation done the next day, and you have to tell her the earliest is two weeks!

"The salesperson said there would be no problem getting it installed. If I'd known it would take this long, I would have bought it from someone else! I may just cancel and do that!"

One of the reasons that we take advantage of our *happy* customers is that we feel more at ease with them. It's much easier to use our skills with unhappy customers, because they are "squeakier wheels."

Super Service recommends that we "oil" both the *happy* and the *unhappy* customer. If we concentrate on using all our communication skills with both types of customer, two things will happen:

1. The happy customer will remain happy. ·
2. The unhappy customer will become happy!

Ten Keys to Handling an Unhappy Customer

When all fired up and angry, a customer doesn't have time to be friendly. So you have to assume the entire responsibility.

> ### Key Point
> Your attitude is contagious. If you hold a friendly space for customers to vent their anger, they will calm down more quickly, and you will feel more in control and professional.

So fight fire with friendliness. On the next page are ten keys to dealing with unhappy customers.

TEN KEYS FOR DEFUSING UNHAPPY CUSTOMERS

1. Show empathy that you understand their situation.

   "I'm sorry."

2. Encourage venting to help them get rid of their anger.

   "Please tell me what happened."

3. Stay objective and don't take it personally.

   "I can understand how you would feel that way."

4. Remain calm to the situation by remaining peaceful.

   "I believe we can resolve this."

5. Listen attentively and show you are listening.

   "Aha, yes, I see."

6. Take responsibility and show urgency.

   "I will make sure this problem is resolved ASAP."

7. Involve the customer in the solution.

   "How would you like this handled?"

8. Give added value.

   "Another way we can help resolve this situation is ..."

9. Provide an action plan.

   "This is what I propose to do ..."

10. Involve your management.

    "I will make management aware of this problem."

Letting the Customer Vent

Let customers vent all their feelings, but do not take them on board. In other words, remain nonemotional: This is not a personal attack. The customer is angry, and that's all there is to it. Here are some tips to use with a venting customer:

Never do these things with venting customers:

- Get angry yourself.
- Tell them to calm down.
- Defend yourself.
- Interrupt.
- Fail to acknowledge their anger.

Do these things with venting customers:

- Listen actively for what they want to happen.
- Allow their rage to burn itself out.
- Visualize them cooling down to green.
- Keep yourself calm by breathing calmly.
- Acknowledge their feelings.

It doesn't matter if customers are right or wrong, they need to air their complaint. If you do not treat them with care, you may lose them completely.

It's as if you are whitewater rafting. Your customer is the raging water, and you are taking great care to steer your raft to calmer waters. You don't allow yourself to get sucked in. Their words flow like water underneath you. Your breathing is calm, and on every exhalation, you let go of your own emotionality. Remember, the customer is simply angry! You could be their mother/father/sibling/best friend/lover/teacher, and they would still be angry.

When a customer is angry, there is nothing you can do except listen. Listening doesn't mean you agree with them; you are acting like a sounding board, and their words bounce off you without inflicting any pain.

One of the keys we mentioned is to accept responsibility. However, it's no good just saying it. You have to take action. On the following page is a tried-and-true recipe for accepting responsibility by taking action.

PLAN FOR TAKING ACTION

1. Write down what the customer says, to show that you are actively listening.

2. Use positive words:

   "Consider it done!"

3. Give your name:

   "My name is _____, and I will take care of this."

4. Show that their issue is your priority:

   "I will have an answer for you today."

5. Thank the customer for the opportunity:

   "Thank you for the opportunity to be of service."

6. Sound confident and responsive:

   "I am confident I can help."

Definitely avoid some phrases when dealing with unhappy customers. Here are some of them:

PHRASES TO AVOID

"I'll get to you in a minute."

"The company policy states ... "

"I've been too busy to ..."

"This never happens normally."

"I'm sorry, that's not my responsibility."

And here are some phrases to use:

PHRASES TO USE

"I will take care of you right away."

"How can I help?"

"It is my responsibility to help find a solution."

"Tell me more about this problem."

"That is quite a problem. I don't blame you for feeling upset."

"I'll make sure this gets corrected right away."

Sometimes when we communicate, we build barriers that stop the information from getting through. The barriers include everything from noise to judgments to prejudices. Here are some ways to overcome such barriers.

WAYS TO OVERCOME BARRIERS

1. Block out surrounding noise by focusing on your customer.

2. Gather knowledge about your company and customers so that you can provide informed solutions.

3. Mirror the customer's nonverbal cues.

4. Actively listen.

5. Don't allow your judgments or prejudices to interfere.

6. Be aware of your tone, posture, and attitude.

The Irate Customer

Sometimes unhappy customers can be savage. They can use foul language, scream, shout, rant, and rave. While it is important not to take their venting personally, taking abuse is part of your job. Here are some simple tactics to calm irate customers:

1. **Visualization.** See them as small, newborn babies screaming for attention and you are the only person around to feed them.

   Tip: Sit tight—they will stop eventually.

2. **Gentle reminder.** Bring them back to sanity by gently saying, "Is there something I have done to personally upset you? I would like to help you. Please give me a chance."

3. **Transfer.** Sometimes the customer is too wild for one person to handle. Say, "I think my manager may be able to help you."

4. **Call security.** If the customer seems likely to turn into a savage beast and become physical, call for security.

CHECK-IN

1. Think of a time when you were an unhappy customer.

   a. Can you remember how you felt?

   b. Did you suffer buyer's remorse?

   c. Were you concerned that the product/service did not meet your needs?

   d. Were you concerned that repairs to the product would cost more than its current value?

   e. Write down any other concerns you had.

   _____

2. How do you like to be handled when you are an unhappy customer?

   a. With a sense of urgency?

   b. Reassured that the problem can be resolved?

   c. That the person is confident and responsive?

   d. That the repairs won't cost more than the product?

   e. _____

Your task is to become aware of how you normally handle unhappy customers. This awareness will help you not only in your business life but in your personal life too.

ACTION

Think of either a happy customer you usually forget about or an unhappy customer you would like to have better customer relations with. What about building the relationship?

1. Choose an internal or external, happy or unhappy customer?

2. If applicable to your job, invite the person for lunch or coffee.

3. Call the customers to update them on new products/services.

4. Send a thank-you card for their business.

5. Think about how you can work together as a team.

Life is too short to hold grudges. Life is too hard to be in combative relationships. You can make the difference; you just need to make the choice.

Chapter 11

SELLING SKILLS

One of the key components of selling is to have great energy.

Super Service providers are also salespeople. You are always selling yourself, your services, or your company. If you think about it, the whole world is a gigantic sales machine. Selling is not just confined to sales and marketing; selling involves every walk of life, including politics, healthcare, school districts, construction, space projects, etc.

As a *Super Service* provider, you can offer your customers better service when you understand the six sales situations that may provide them with a solution:

1. The service/product does not fit the customer's needs.
2. An additional part/process/program/piece is needed to make the product/service function properly.
3. The product or service is out of date.
4. A new upgrade will enhance the product/service.
5. The customer has outgrown the product/service.
6. A competitive system/product is incompatible with yours.

Not all service situations can be answered by a sale. In some situations selling is a definite no-no! Here are four examples:

1. Your product/service does not and will never meet the customer's needs.
2. The product/service created a big problem for them and they want to stay mad.
3. An upgrade provides no additional benefit
4. The product/service is defective and needs to be exchanged.

What *can* you do in such situations?

The OPEN Technique

Selling is the ability to get commitment from people to say yes to products or services. As a *Super Service* provider you have the opportunity to up-sell, and we want to give you the very best technique. The sales technique is called OPEN, an acronym for a series of questions that enable the *Super Service* provider to identify the customer's needs. The technique can be easily learned and used in any situation. Here is the basic formula:

O **Opening questions.** Start the sale by understanding the background.

P **Probing questions.** Reveal problems, difficulty, or dissatisfaction.

E **Extend questions.** Explode the problems into other areas.

N **Net gain questions.** Develop solutions that address needs.

Opening Questions

Let's say your product does not fit the customer's needs. Your first job is to gather background information. It doesn't matter if you are in the clothing business ("What kind of function are you attending?") or scrap metal ("How do you organize your scrap recovery?"). An opening question gives you background information that will help you uncover the customer's need.

Safe

It is safe to ask opening questions with new customers, either early in the conversation or when the customer's situation has changed.

Hazardous

It is hazardous to ask opening questions late in the conversation, in sensitive areas, or when you sound like an interrogator by asking too many.

Probing Questions

Once you understand the background, you need to know the specific problem. If you work for a car manufacturing company it could be, "What kind of quality issues do you experience?" For a food wholesaler, the question might be, "Is there any part of your operation that is costing you too much money?" A probing question begins to examine areas where your customer is experiencing problems.

Safe

It is safe to ask probing questions early in the conversation, in areas where your product or service can provide solutions, or in areas that are significant to your customer.

Hazardous

It is hazardous to ask probing questions in sensitive areas such as where organizational politics run high, where the customer has a high personal or emotional involvement, or where your product/service does not provide a solution.

Extend Questions

If you know the problem, you can explode it into other areas to create an even greater need: "What effect does this situation have on your delivery system?" "How do the breakdowns impact employee morale?" An extend question helps customers realize that the problem reaches into other areas. It gives them additional reasons for seeking a solution.

Safe

It is safe to ask extend questions when problems are significant and complex.

Hazardous

It is hazardous to ask extend questions too early in the conversation or in situations that you cannot solve.

Net Gain Questions

Customers buy because they have needs. Net gain questions help the customer realize the gain of your solution. Again, it doesn't matter if you work for a banqueting service ("If you save 10 cents a plate, how much would that mean in total savings?") or for a swimming pool manufacturer ("How much would the self-clean process reduce your maintenance costs?").

Safe

It is safe to ask net gain questions when they pay off in other areas or when the solutions must be justified by the customer.

Hazardous

It is hazardous to ask net gain questions too early in the conversation.

Energy

One of the key components of selling is to have great energy. Let's look at a case study in energy. A construction company we consult with has the best receptionist we've ever met. She sells her company just by her upbeat energy. Her name is Barbara and we asked how she does it:

One of my main motivations for responding to callers in an enthusiastic and gracious manner is quite simply because that's the way I like to be treated. There is nothing more unappealing than to call a business office and have the person answer the phone sounding as if they are doing you a favor by answering your call.

Another motivation is selfishness. When I act in a positive, cheerful manner, people usually respond to me accordingly. Others often start to mirror my enthusiastic demeanor. All of us have days when we feel lethargic and less lively than others. But if you act as though you were energetic and positive, you start to feel that way. You start to fool people into believing you feel great! That's what I try to do.

People often perceive the receptionist to be merely the person who picks up a ringing telephone. The job is considered by many to be uncreative and routine. On the contrary, I think of it as the first opportunity to make a good and memorable impression on a customer or a potential customer. By interacting positively with all types of personalities, from all walks of life, the receptionist is constantly creating a rapport and a relationship for his or her company.

Here are the main points for having great energy:

1. Be enthusiastic and gracious.
2. Act in a positive and cheerful manner.
3. In a front-line job, make the first impression good and memorable.
4. Create a good rapport and relationship with the customer.

In comparison, our salesperson, Carol, focuses on being assertive and persistent—persistent in a professional sense. It doesn't mean being rude or obnoxious and calling all the time. Carol believes that she has something worthwhile to say and do, and her energy conveys that message to her customers.

Here's what Carol says about her job:

My motto is, I might not be seeing you this month, but I will be seeing you! If a company has a need for our service, it becomes like a game. "All I want is 20 minutes of your time. I believe we have an outstanding service; if you give me that 20 minutes, I'll show you how we can help you to increase sales, have happier, more motivated employees, and satisfy 100% of your customers, 100% of the time!"

If Carol took rejection personally, she would not be able to do her job. Often, she gets rejected, treated without respect, told to call back next month or next year.

Energy for Selling

1. **Persistence:** "I'm here to make an appointment with you, and it's going to happen sooner or later."

2. **Focus:** "I know what I want from this call, and I will keep directing it back to my goal."

3. **Assertive:** "I know how much our services have helped other companies like yours; we just want the opportunity to discuss your needs."

4. **Energy:** "I don't take rejection personally. I move on to the next call."

Here's how Carol's persistence worked with U.S. Robotics before they became 3Com. She had driven past their company and wanted to do business with them. She got the name of the person she needed to talk with and called. She called every day and got either the person's assistant or voice mail. Carol would come into the office and before she even took off her coat, she dialed the number, and she would dial it at different times throughout the day. One day we said to her, "Don't tell us you're still trying to get in there!" We all laughed.

Finally, Carol was told the person had left the company. That still didn't stop her. Carol kept calling until she was given another name. Five calls later she got through to another person and was immediately given an appointment. It took 347 calls over a 10-month period. Now that they have seen the kind of work we do, they have become one of our major customers.

As Carol says, "One of two things has to happen: They either give me the appointment, or they have to tell me to stop calling!"

CHECK-IN

Next time you are selling, consider this list of skills:

1. Be able to maintain an enthusiastic and positive attitude.

2. Want to do the best for the customer.

3. Know the basic selling skills.

4. Want the customer to be left with a great lasting impression.

5. Be aware of both the internal and external customers.

To be a great salesperson you need to have:

1. Persistence, assertiveness, focus, energy.

2. Objectivity—don't take rejection personally.

3. Belief in your product or service.

Chapter 12

TELEPHONE SKILLS

In the business world the phone is like a screwdriver.
It can open things, close things, and it can also screw things up.

People will make assumptions about you, just by your telephone skills. So here are a couple of tips right off the bat:

1. Return calls immediately.

2. Keep messages short, and include the response you need.

One manager we know fast-forwards to the end of long-winded messages; any vital information in the middle is lost. If you're guilty of leaving endless phone messages, here's what to do: Call yourself and leave a lengthy message. Play it back, jot down three key points, and turn it into *one* short sentence. Call yourself again and leave the shortened message. Play it back and notice the difference.

Here's another exercise. *Highlight the key phrase in this message:*

My name is Brown, my number is 900-3000 and I need an estimate for a model 60 unit. I need to update it because I've had the older version, which I got from your competitor, for over three years. It's time for a new one! I heard about your company from a friend of mine and they were very happy with your product and service. It seems that the new plastic coating works well in my type of environment. I work in a—well, I can tell you about that when you return my call (ha, ha). I'm in the building from 8:00 A.M. to 5:00 P.M. (I try to get out by 4:00 P.M., but not today—worst luck). My lunch hour is twelve 'til one. If I'm not here when you call, please leave a message, and I will get right back to you. Oh, I'd also like to know about any volume discounts. There are some other people who may be interested. People in finance and H.R., but we can talk about that when you call. Look forward to hearing from you. Again my number is 900-3000 and my name is Brown! Thanks, and have a great day!"

Get to the point! Name, number, and the reason for the call. The first sentence said it all.

The Effect of Your Voice

Your voice sounds different from other people's. It is unique to you and reflects your personality and inner attitude. If you are angry you will sound angry. Voices can be annoying or pleasant to listen to. They can be clear, squeaky, difficult to decipher, monotonous, low-pitched, or high-pitched.

Four factors determine how your voice sounds:

- Rate of speech
- Volume
- Tone
- Diction

The energy you put into your voice reflects your attitude, enthusiasm, and willingness to serve. If you are soft-spoken, it can seem as though you don't know what you are talking about. If you are loud, you can seem overbearing. Adjust the volume of your voice to your customer's volume unless, of course, the customer is shouting and angry!

Choose words that can be easily understood. Be caring and confident. Speak at a rate that is neither too fast nor too slow. The following passage is 140 words in length. Using the second hand of your watch, time yourself while you read it aloud:

There is no set rule for the rate of speaking of individuals. Some persons can speak at a rate of one hundred ninety words per minute and be clearly understood, while others must speak as slowly as ninety words per minute to achieve the same understanding. Most experts feel, however, that there is more to be gained by **speaking slowly.** *They have decided that a rate of about one hundred forty words per minute is a safe rate. The main disadvantage of speaking too fast is that you cannot be understood easily. Speaking too fast has other disadvantages. Your client may get the impression of being high-pressured into something. In addition, your client may get the impression that you are very rushed and concerned with time. To be really understood, we recommend that you speak slowly.* **One hundred forty!** **One forty!**

The Faceless Voice on the Line

Here's another phone phenomenon: You have no idea (unless you're on a video conference call) what the other persons are doing, who they're with, or where they are. With call forwarding, they could be on another continent.

We know a person who took his business to Florida and never told any customers. If there was a problem, he'd fly in, take care of it, and fly out again. Never make assumptions with the telephone.

You could be talking about someone who is standing right next to the person you're calling. Have you ever done this? A person with a loud voice calls, you have to hold the phone away from your ear, and everyone in the room hears!

Don't be paranoid about the phone, but do treat it with respect. In the business world the phone is like a screwdriver: It can open things, close things, and screw things up.

Your Effectiveness on the Phone

Ask yourself this: Do I help my customers? Do I use empathy and understanding? Do I sleep at night knowing that I've done the best job I could do? Here are some affirmations to help you prepare.

SUPER SERVICE AFFIRMATIONS

1. **My customer is anyone who isn't me!**

2. I keep an open mind.

3. I allow people to speak.

4. I repeat their message for clear understanding.

5. I keep my tone light.

6. I sit up straight.

7. I concentrate on the conversation.

8. I smile when I dial.

9. I vary my pace.

10. I stay interested.

11. I answer by the second or third ring.

12. I provide my company name and department.

13. I give my name.

14. I ask, "How may I help you?"

15. I am courteous.

16. I am willing.

17. I am giving.

18. I take responsibility.

19. I am friendly.

20. I enjoy the telephone.

HOW TO TRANSFER A CALL

T **Take** time to communicate:

"Linda in accounts will be able to answer your question."

R **Request** permission:

"May I add Linda to our call?"

A **Add** calls while remaining on the line:

"I'll stay on the line until Linda joins our call."

N **Never** use the term "transfer":

"Linda will be added to our call. Is that all right?"

S **Stay** on the line until the problem is resolved:

"Thank you for holding. This is Linda from accounts, Mr. Bachman; I've explained your problem to her. Linda, this is Mr. Bachman."

F **Focus** on solving all the customer's issues:

"Is there anything else that I can help you with today?"

E **Empathize** with your customers:

"I know how frustrating this must have been for you. I hope the problem has been resolved to your satisfaction."

R **Remember** you can make this a great experience:

"I'm very pleased to be of service. Is there anything else I can help you with?"

HOW TO TAKE AN ACCURATE MESSAGE

- Record the time and date on a message pad.

- Ask for the company name, the caller's name, and the telephone number.

- Ask for and write the message clearly.

- Repeat all of the above for accuracy.

- Ask for the best time to return the call.

- State, "I will give her the message."

- Sign the message.

- Place the message where it can be clearly seen (or leave it in voice/e-mail if the person is not available).

Using the Phone with a Computer

We consulted with a customer service department for a large marine company. The customer service providers sit with phone terminals in their ears, looking at a computer screen. They deal with agents who purchase their equipment.

They need the agent's number to access all their information on screen. The customer care people are so focused on getting the agent's number that the first words out of their mouth are, "What's your number?" Even angry customers are greeted with, "What's your number?"

Has that happened to you? It's like being discounted. A better way to answer calls is to listen to at least one or two sentences of the customer's problem. Then, when you have some understanding of the issues, say, "I understand your problem. May I have your agent number so I can help you by seeing all your information on my screen?"

Management has the philosophy that if they get the call rate as high as possible, they are providing good customer care. In reality, all that's happening is that their figures look good.

Chapter 13

HOW TO AVOID STRESS AND BURNOUT

You can forsee stress.
You can forsee burnout.
You can plan how to handle them.

Imagine a high-wire performer. Halfway through the act, the wire gets so stressed it snaps and the performer falls.

Imagine a forest. A blazing fire spreads out of control and burns every tree (including mature redwoods and young saplings).

The high-wire performer wasn't stressed, and the forest didn't start the fire; however, both suffered as a result of coming into contact with stress and burnout.

Fortunately, you are neither a high-wire performer nor a tree. You don't have to stand completely still or take terrifying risks. You are a *Super Service* provider—a professional whose job is to deal with customers.

Customers are your potential wires and fires. Even though they are not part of you, they can affect you so that you feel stressed and burned out. This happens when you ignore the signals.

A wise person once said, "God always sends pebbles before the rocks." So the best way to avoid stress and burnout is to take notice of the pebbles.

Key Point
A high-wire performer who knows the wire is already stressed will not walk it. If you know your customer is already stressed, do not talk it! (Let them vent.)

The Stress and Burnout Scenario

We have given you many *Super Service* tips on how to relieve stress and burnout—breathing, taking a break, or repeating affirmations. In this chapter, we are going beyond tips. Here, we are giving you keys to *prevent* stress and burnout from happening in the first place. First, let's take a close look at the cause of stress and burnout.

Let's say you are having a so-so day, not bad, not good. You get an irate customer; you handle it. Your boss is angry; you handle it. You get another angry customer; you handle it. A coworker wants help with a problem she should be able to solve by now; you handle it. You have lunch, the food is terrible, and everyone is talking about a TV show you didn't see. You feel isolated.

Back on the job, your boss is after you for something that wasn't your fault; you take it personally! Another customer calls with a complaint. You don't have the authority to solve it, so you pass it along to your manager who is annoyed at the disruption.

It's nearing the end of your day, and your boss asks you to stay and finish something up. Finally, you leave work. You feel miserable.

By the time you get home, you feel:

- *Either* lonely because no one is around,
- *or* confined because too many people are around.
- *Either* upset because there's no one to talk to,
- *or* frustrated because you have to listen to others' problems.
- *Either* depressed because you have nothing to do,
- *or* anxious because you have too much to do.

Whatever your scenario, you feel miserable. You wake up the next day, say an affirmation, and go to work. The same things happen—angry boss, irate customers, inconsiderate coworkers.

This scenario continues until it becomes a chronic situation. You are drowning in an ongoing cycle of stress and burnout. You feel the only way out is to get another job.

You find a new job, but soon the same things start happening. You become so stressed and so burned out that you decide on a complete life change. You buy a plane ticket and fly away to a beautiful island and get a new job.

Life is great for the first few months. Then you notice a person who is angry, just like your old boss used to be! Your coworkers leave you out of conversations. Your customers complain for no reason. Stress and burnout are in your life whatever way you turn!

We've deliberately painted the worst-case scenario. All the same, maybe one or two things strike a chord with you and you do experience stress and burnout from time to time.

Let's get back to the high-wire performer and the forest. What do these two things have in common?

Answer: The stress and burnout had nothing to do with them. They just happened to be in the path. They felt at the mercy of the wire or the fire.

Do you see how that happens? The high-wire performer was just doing what high-wire people do. The forest was just being a forest. Then along came stress and burnout, and both were destroyed in the path.

Coping with Frustration

If you are really angry at someone, the only person that you can be sure is really suffering is you.

It's like the breakup of a relationship. One partner usually feels the hurt more than the other. While the unhappy person is ranting and raving about his lost partner, the lost partner is happily taking care of herself. For most of us, voodoo dolls don't work, except on ourselves! When we feel anger and hatred, *we are the ones feeling it*. We are the ones being hurt. If this does not sound true, think about it for a moment. If there is conflict in your life, who is creating it? Whether the conflict is between yourself and another person or within your department, if you are not creating it, you are probably feeding it! There is no one else.

The solution is to let go of our feelings and serve the customer. It doesn't mean that you must lose your own identity, or that you are "stuck" with someone else in your space. We have free choice to move where and when we will.

Control Your Environment

Let's go back to the work scenario. The angry boss, the irate customer, the inconsiderate coworkers, the inadequate home life—all these things are out-side your control.

Or are they? Our friend Mary works as an advertising copy writer. Mary is of short stature. At 41 inches (3 feet 5 inches), she is about the same height as a three-year-old child. Mary walks with the aid of crutches, drives a car, is always bright and cheerful, and has one of the most positive attitudes on the planet. Could she be stressed or burned out? Absolutely. It takes longer for her to walk places. She depends on strangers to open and close doors, push elevator buttons, and on and on. Intrigued about her stress and burnout levels, we asked her if we could interview her for this chapter. She said yes!

Gees: Do you ever feel stressed and burned out?

Mary: Oh, yes. It can be very stressful at times.

Gees: But you always seem so happy; how do you avoid the stress and burnout?

Mary: I visualize the situation I'm going into. I foresee possible stressful situations and I address those fears beforehand. It's like heading them off at the pass.

Gees: Can you give us an example?

Mary: If I'm meeting with a client, I think of ways to not make bad things happen. I call a cab way in advance so that I get there on time. I call to find out if the place is accessible or, if not, whether they can have someone assist me. I introduce myself over the phone and make friends with that person beforehand.

Gees: Anything else?

Mary: I always give myself a reward when I've gone through it.

Gees: How do your customers handle your being a little person?

Mary: I used to not tell them that I was 41 inches tall, but I found it shocked some customers. Others would say, "I wish I had known: I would have done this or that for you." For example, one customer now has a cushion in her car, so that I can sit higher up.

Gees: So making the customer comfortable helps your stress level?

Mary: Oh, yes. I always do research ahead of time. I find the "vibe" of the office. How are things run? What is their culture? Then I fit in with them.

Gees: What happens when you meet a customer for the first time?

Mary: I had Montgomery Ward as a client and I was dealing with their fashion buyers in New York. Eventually I went there on a business trip and one of the men I had talked with every day on the phone invited me to a show and dinner. I asked all my friends, should I tell him about my stature or not? Some said yes, some said no. I ended up telling him and he was confused at first, and then said, fine, he was 6 feet 4 inches tall. We had a great time, he carried my purse.

Key Point
Mary foresees stressful situations and takes care of them before they arise. Then she rewards herself for having done a good job.

You may think that your situation is not so simple, that you don't have time to plan and organize the way Mary does. Your customers come at you hard and fast. Sometimes you can't duck! You don't have time to visualize the situation. You can't head them off at the pass.

This is not true! If you have been in your job for a few days, you know what kind of customers you have. You know what kind of boss you have. You know what kind of coworkers you have. You *can* foresee situations. You *can* foresee stress. You *can* foresee burnout. You *can* plan how to handle them.

The problem is that most of us take everything so personally. We see ourselves as at the mercy of other people. The high-wire breaks and we fall. The fire blazes and we burn. If we remember that we do not have to walk the wire or stand in the path of a blazing fire, we can avoid the stress and burnout. Here are some tips.

Rules for Avoiding Stress and Burnout
1. Identify the stressful situation.
2. Identify solutions.
3. Plan how to bring your solutions into effect.
4. Plan your reward.

CHECK-IN

Use one sentence to describe the most stressful situation in your job at this moment:

_____

_____

Write out two solutions that will help the situation:

1. _____

2. _____

Choose the most effective solution that will bring the strongest and most lasting results. Explain, in 10 words or less, how and when you plan putting this into practice.

_____

_____

_____

_____

Write down your reward. Choose something that you really enjoy, that doesn't cost a lot of money or take too much time.

_____

_____

A SUPER SERVICE PRAYER

May I walk with the desire to serve

May I open my heart to the needs of others

That my soul will leap in the joy of helping

That my circle of friends will grow with harmony

May I feel at one with the universe, one song for all

That my ego be fulfilled in the service of others

That my needs be filled by the joy of assisting

That my wants are turned into giving

And my desires turned into golden caring

May abundance of health, wealth, and happiness be mine

Coming from this desire to serve

This openness of heart

This joy of soul

Thank you, wondrous creator, for all my blessings

And may I learn to count them every day

And know that I am never alone.

Super Service—Final Words to End on ...

You decide how you are going to live your life all the time. Every day you have choices on which way you want to go. You have the power to make or break organizations. You are the value-added. Your attitude, the way you come to work every day, the things you do—that's what makes the difference.

As soon as you become conscious, aware, and focused, wonderful things begin to happen. It's the strange thing of life; the buck actually stops at you. We have this strange notion that senior people know more than we do, but they are sitting in their office wondering what to do. They need communication to go forward, so it's back to, what do you bring to the table? Are you walking the walk?

Is it better when it comes from management down? Yes, it's much better when it comes down. Most people need direction. We need to know where we are going. What are you contributing as an individual? What is your attitude when you walk to work every day? Are you contributing to the positive side or the negative side? What did you do to invest your time towards a good purpose? We are all in favor of having things stuck around your office or cubicle to help you remember you are a human being, that you are here to serve and be the best you can be.

We would like to leave you with a little reminder. When you deliver *Super Service*, the person feeling the best is you. So what is one thing, starting tomorrow morning, that you can do every day that will make a difference? Remember, one small step for you—one huge leap for *Super Service*.

INDEX

INDEX

About the Authors

Jeff Gee is a motivational speaker and master trainer with Motorola. He has over 30 years' experience in the business world and founded McNeil and Johnson in 1982, a management training company. Jeff wrote and self-published *Strategies for Winning*, a manual and set of six audio tapes that sold over 20,000 copies. Jeff Gee trains and motivates groups of people almost every day. He travels regularly to Asia, Europe, Eastern Europe, South America, Australia, and extensively throughout the United States.

Val Gee is an educational specialist and ordained priest. Val has had over 10 articles published in *Training* magazine entitled "Insight."

Their various (self-published) training manuals have sold over 20,000 copies. The authors have an extensive client list that includes Siemens, Motorola, Abbott & Culligan International, 3COM, Platinum Technology, Crane International, Pitney Bowes, Baxter, Sears, and Hyatt Hotels.